DATE DUE			

The Competent Woman

IRVINGTON SOCIAL RELATIONS SERIES

General Editor: David C. McClelland, Harvard University

Rosalind C. Barnett & Grace K. Baruch: *The Competent Woman* (1978)

Daniel Goleman: *The Varieties of the Meditative Experience* (1978)

Richard deCharms: *Enhancing Motivation* (1976)

David C. McClelland: *Power* (1975)

The Competent Woman
PERSPECTIVES ON DEVELOPMENT

by

Rosalind C. Barnett and Grace K. Baruch

with an Afterword
by Carolyn G. Heilbrun

IRVINGTON PUBLISHERS, INC., New York

**HALSTED PRESS Division of
JOHN WILEY & SONS**

New York   London   Sydney   Toronto

For our families

R.C.B.

G.K.B.

Copyright © 1978 by Rosalind C. Barnett and Grace K. Baruch

Distributed by HALSTED PRESS
A division of JOHN WILEY & SONS, New York

Library of Congress Cataloging in Publication Data
Barnett, Rosalind C.
  The competent woman.

  Bibliography: p.
  Includes index.
  1. Women—Psychology. 2. Socialization.
3. Success. 4. Ability. I. Baruch, Grace K.,
joint author. II. Title.
HQ1206.B26 1978 155.6'33 78-8380
ISBN 0-470-26424-1

Printed in the United States of America

Preface

In this book we present an overview of issues relevant to the development of competence in women, drawing from a variety of sources--experimental and anecdotal, technical and non-technical, empirical and theoretical. Our goal is to introduce the non-specialist to a body of knowledge reflecting the contributions of many disciplines, including of course our own--psychology. Our audience is thus comprised not only of those interested in psychology but also those interested in such topics as the family, education, and women's studies. This book should also be of interest to women concerned with shaping their own lives, and to parents and professionals who influence the lives of girls and women.

The concept of competence, defined briefly here as the ability to interact effectively with the "real world," provides a useful framework for diverse topics. Of particular concern are the social and psychological obstacles that women must often surmount in order to become, and believe themselves to be, competent.

In the first chapter we discuss the nature of competence. We review what is known about successful women in Chapter 2 and next look specifically and separately at the influences of fathers (Chapter 3) and mothers (Chapter 4). Analysis of the impact of various marital and family patterns comes in Chapter 5. In Chapter 6, we examine the roles of schools and the educational structure; in Chapter 7, attitudes related to achievement.

Several aspects of our book require comment. First, the greater part of our material is concerned with white women, particularly those of middle-class origins. No doubt our own status as white middle-class women in part determined this focus; we are not well-equipped to address the situation of black women, who so often play the role of economic provider and whose lives are shaped by many forces that diverge greatly from those influencing whites--and this too in ways that are relevant to the development of competence.* Patricia Harris (1974), the first black woman to be made a member of the Cabinet, states:

> One of the little appreciated results of the black experience has been an anticipation by a significant part of the black middle class of the life style now sought by white middle-class women in the woman's liberation movement...There was general acceptance by the black community that women would work and that the better educated the woman, the less demeaning the work (p. 16).

Second, we devote the greater part of our attention to forms of competence traditionally associated with males, because these forms are also associated with social value, social rewards, and power. In hunter-gatherer societies, for example, where women gathered wild fruits and nuts and men hunted for meat, perhaps 90% of the nutritional needs of the group were supplied by what the women gathered; yet

*The sociologist Sara Lightfoot (1976) deplores the lack of information about the development of black women: "Young black girls are an ignored and invisible population."

meat, and the hunting skills that provided it, were more highly valued. In our own society too, the inequality in social rewards consistently favors the work men do and the skills and traits associated with their endeavors. We shall be paying more attention, therefore, to women who are scholars, lawyers, surgeons, and business managers than to nurses, school teachers, or ballerinas.

Finally, we consider ourselves to be "feminists" in that we believe fully in the goals of the women's movement: to reject old constraints, to make women aware of the conditions that limit their life choices, and to ensure that women are no longer barred from access to high-level positions in any social institutions. As supporters of this movement we hold that being feminine and being powerful can go together. Many people, women as well as men, are not yet ready to accept this view. They tell women, as they have told black people, that it is a great blessing to be outside the rat race characteristic of middle-class American life and (in a change of metaphor) that since the pie is rotten, fighting for pieces of it is a misguided effort.

On the grounds that such arguments ask a woman to renounce what is not yet available to her, we reject them. One can freely choose a way of life only when other ways are possible. Arguments against equality for women that rest on devaluing "establishment-oriented" institutions as competitive and aggressive can be used to obscure actual discrimination and social injustice. The "rotten pie" argument is often used not only by men who would not think of removing themselves or their sons from the race for conventional forms of success, but by women who continue to encourage their husbands and sons in these same pursuits.

Thus one need not necessarily endorse the values and·goals of contemporary American culture to advocate that women be equipped to compete on its terms if they so choose. Moreover, the reform of destructive aspects of a society is most effectively carried out by its influential members. In the following chapters, therefore, we try to show the ways, both obvious and subtle, in which limitations on women are perpetuated and, perhaps more important, to indicate how the different parts of society may be opened up to all people. In the bewildering metaphoric language of the opposition, we think it possible that by entering the rat race, women may change the rules of the game, the nature of the prize, and the quality of the pie!

We value highly the comments of colleagues who read all or portions of this manuscript during its preparation: Patricia Graham, Susan Lloyd, David McClelland, Joseph Pleck, David Tyack, Mary Roth Walsh, Joyce Walstedt. The warm encouragement and tactful suggestions of Carolyn Heilbrun supported us long before we had the good fortune of her consent to provide an Afterword. Combining personal interest and professional skills, Franklin Baruch provided an extraordinarily painstaking and invaluable critique.

The skillful work of Joanne Robinson, Jeanne Klainer, and Erica West in typing successive versions of the manuscript greatly facilitated our efforts. We are also indebted to Kay Bruner, our copy editor, whose stylistic good sense added greatly to this book. To a great extent this book would not have been possible without my (RB) having had the opportunity and privilege of working with Professor Renato Tagiuri and learning from him the skills of writing and organization. Nor would it have been possible without the encouragement that has been shown to us by Professor Lotte Bailyn.

Rosalind Barnett
Grace Baruch

Contents

		Page
Dedication		iv
Preface		v
I.	The Nature of Competence	13
II.	Successful Women	22
III.	Fathers and Daughters	51
IV.	Mothers and Daughters	69
V.	Marital and Family Patterns: Themes and Variations	88
VI.	Schools and Competence	107
VII.	Achievement: Attitudes, Beliefs, Motives	131
Afterword		152
Bibliography		158
Index		175

The Competent Woman

I. The Nature of Competence

What is Competence?

A glance at the Book Review section of the Sunday *New York Times* clearly reveals the eagerness of Americans to acquire any and all kinds of skills. A typical issue includes a wide variety of "how-to" books, from gardening, to living to a ripe old age and enjoying it, to raising children, to repairing one's car. Clearly we are a nation in search of ways to feel skillful, to achieve, to compete--in short, to acquire competence.

Dictionaries tell us that a competent person is one who is capable, fit, adequate, qualified. But they do not say capable of what--programing a computer, bearing a child, canning vegetables, quilting, curing illness? Not all forms of competence are equally valued by society; and even those forms highly valued at one time and place may be devalued at another.

We usually call competent those people who do well what they set out to do, effectively organizing human and material resources to achieve, create, or produce a socially valued service or product. Such people both work to realize certain goals of the society, and expect their effort to bring rewards-- social recognition, heightened self-esteem, financial renumeration. In their discussion of the growth of competence, Kevin Connolly and Jerome Bruner (1974) point out that, "In any given society, there are a set of skills which are essential for coping with existing realities, but not every member of a society will have all skills" (p. 4). Indeed, a major influence in determining what skills one will develop, as we shall see, is one's sex.

The psychologist Robert White (1959) has argued that human beings are characterized by a basic motivation to be competent, to interact effectively with the environment. Adaptation and survival are heavily dependent on this interaction, as is the ability to learn from experience through a process of feedback about the effects of one's actions. Thus the acquisition of competence is described by Connolly and Bruner as a cycle beginning with the selection of those features in the environment that provide information about successes and failures, and going on to use that information to generate new plans. Competence, in short, refers to a basic human need that is channeled into particular forms through the physical and social environment.

Social Influences on Competence

The forms of competence important in early life are similar for both males and females. Infants try to reach and grasp, then walk and talk. Ages for acquiring these skills vary, depending upon maturation, on interactions with other people, and possibly on innate differences in the inherent pleasure each activity provides. One of the basic functions of a parent or caretaker is to provide the stability and reassurance that facilitate exploration of novel activities and environmental features and thus foster the acquisition of competence (Bruner, 1974).

Increasingly, through the life cycle, the development of competence is shaped by what people who are significant in one's life expect, reward, punish, and value. These in turn depend upon one's society, one's social role, and thus one's sex. It can happen that the forms of competence assigned by society to particular groups are inadequate for establishing or maintaining an inner sense of competence in the individual. Take the case of many present-day mothers. Why do skills such as those required for good child-rearing fail to provide so many modern women with a sense of competence? A look at the social influences on competence helps solve the puzzle. In labor-scarce societies where children are a highly valued resource, the ability to bear and rear a child has great social value--greater than in an overpopulated, under-employed society, even though the skills involved do not change radically. Where children are not socially valued, furthermore, the woman whose life is focused on them may exist in a void with respect to feedback about success and failure; what is not valued is ignored. Under such conditions a mother's competent performance is not linked to the life of the society; it carries no message of success or failure, or knowledge of competence.

The increasing incidence of depression in women, especially in those with young children (Radloff, 1975), may be a consequence. Despite the heavy demands on them, many women are isolated from those forms of interaction with the environment necessary for well-being. Information-processing, Robert White (1959) argues, is necessary to the survival of human beings and is innately motivated and inherently pleasureable. A state of cognitive deprivation, such as is characteristic of isolated housewives, and the absence of opportunities to exercise skills, thus create boredom, frustration, and ultimately depression, and in the process inhibit the growth of competence. It is distressing to note in this connection the results of a longitudinal study of changes in IQ with age: the higher a man's score as a child, the more he gained in IQ with age; the higher a woman's score as a child, the less she gained (Kangas & Bradway, 1971). Since the women with lower scores showed a pattern similiar to that of men, it is likely that the conditions of women's lives rather than biological factors explain these results.

Thus, at mid-life many mature women who have lived traditional lives as wives and mothers find themselves ill-equipped to deal with an array of personal and social changes. Some are able to face such predictable events as the increasing independence of their children and to find alternate foci for their energies and skills. But others are overtaken by unpredictable events: an unemployed spouse, divorce, widowhood. These events often cause such women to reassess their established patterns, creating in them a desire and/or need for financial productivity and economic independence.

Yet many women who think about returning to work or to school are beset by a lack of confidence that is almost paralyzing, for acquisition of new goals in the absence of clear means to those goals can be very distressing. Indeed, many women question not only their ability to undertake new projects successfully but the very legitimacy of any plans that might be seen as "selfish." And because the skills they have exercised in the domestic sphere do not usually constitute a source of capital readily transferable to the world of work, women often perceive themselves as less competent than they really are.

Self-Perceptions and Competence

In thinking about what kind of person one is--how good, how competent--no one is completely accurate and objective. Self-perceptions are affected by hopes and fears, wishes and conflicts. For women, however, misperceptions are remarkably consistent in one direction; women tend to underestimate themselves, particularly their abilities and performance, to "assume incompetence" (Vaughter, Gubernick, Mastossian, & Haslett, 1974) compared with their own abilities.

A dramatic contrast is apparent when one turns to males. In a large-scale study of college seniors, for example, Leonard Baird and his colleagues (1973) found that young men who had C+ averages believed they were perfectly capable of earning Ph.D.'s; women with B+ averages did not. The same pattern emerges in studies of athletes' evaluations of their performance (Clifton & Smith, 1963), elementary school children's estimates of their ability to do college work (Wylie, 1963), and college students' predictions of course grades (Vaughter, et al., 1974). Baird (1976) followed up his subjects a year later and found that behavior was consistent with attitudes: women who had had A to A+ grades were no more likely to be attending graduate or professional schools than were men with B grades.

How are we to understand this pattern?[1] Relevant here is M. Brewster Smith's (1968) conceptualization of "the competent self," the attitude toward the self "that orients one to make the most of one's opportunities in the world" (p. 281). This concept has two components: (a) a favorable self-evaluation, or self-respect; and (b) a sense of potency, activity, and efficacy. The former can be seen as self-esteem, the latter as a sense of competence, and they are intertwined. A woman (or man) who lacks a sense of competence is likely to have low self-esteem (Baruch, 1973).

Self-esteem, meaning a favorable overall self-evaluation, is even more difficult to measure than to define; in tests people are usually asked to agree or disagree with statements assumed to reflect their sense of self-worth: e.g., "I wish I could have more respect for myself," (Rosenberg, 1965), or "I am about as attractive as most people I know" (Coopersmith, 1968). In a major study of self-esteem and its antecedents,

Stanley Coopersmith identified four bases by which people judge their self-worth: (a) power--the ability to influence or control others; (b) virtue--adherence to moral and ethical standards; (c) acceptance--affection and attention from others; and (d) competence--successful performance in meeting demands for achievement. People vary in the value they put on each basis. A person we admire for some great achievement may actually have extremely low self-esteem because he or she values acceptance over performance, and feels it lacking.

The socialization of women has been oriented toward virtue and acceptance, not toward power and competence, the double-bind impact of which has often been noted. Society rewards and values those who are powerful and competent, giving little more than lip service to those who are loved and ethical. Women who seek power and competence, thus gaining in two of the bases, often lose in areas of virtue and acceptance, particularly if they fail to consider others before themselves.

The two major requirements for self-esteem, according to Orville Brim (1976), are a feeling of being positively valued by others and a sense of mastery over one's environment. Since women have been persuaded that their value to others may be lessened with the adoption of attitudes and behaviors that promote mastery and a sense of competence, they are in the classic situation of Scylla and Charybdis.

As to a sense of competence, the second component of the "competent self," M. Brewster Smith (1968) has proposed three prerequisites: opportunity, respect, and power. Opportunity provides a feeling of hopefulness about the future; respect from others is necessary for self-respect; and power is what insures respect and opportunity. The consequence of a lack of the first is hopelessness; of the second, self-hatred; and of the third, vulnerability and dependence. Yet in the lives of most women today, there are deficiencies in all three prerequisites. Opportunities have been limited; the family into which a daughter is born does not think of her as a potential leader. Respect is ensured neither by living out the traditional role of wife and mother nor by declining to do so. Most central is the question of power. Being powerful and being feminine have been in our society well-nigh mutually exclusive. Indeed, in terms of their authority or legitimized power, women have been in all known societies less powerful than men, although they have often been influential (Rosaldo & Lamphere, 1974).

A uniquely feminine dilemma is that these three elements of a sense of competence are often in conflict; most often, the conflict is between respect on the one hand and opportunity and power on the other. In the traditional female role pattern, the respect and approval of one's loved ones are what count, a goal attained often at the cost of renouncing opportunity and power (and opportunities for power) in order to put family before self and, on another level, to avoid criticism and conflict. Rarely is the development of such qualities as leadership, self-reliance, and independence consistent with traditional concepts of the good wife and mother. Although under special circumstances--when the husband must be away for long periods of time, to earn a living or to fight a war--these traditionally masculine qualities may be temporarily commended to women, they are meant to be shed upon the husband's return. Thus women have tended neither to develop competence-related traits nor to perceive themselves as having these qualities. Attributes such as assertiveness and independence, indeed, are considered signs of masculinity, in conflict with those of femininity--nurturance, consideration for others, gentleness.

Research on self-perceptions and traits related to sex roles has revealed that socially valued traits tend to form a competence cluster and to be associated with males (Broverman, Vogel, Broverman, Clarkson, & Rosenkrantz, 1972). In this study women perceived themselves as relatively deficient in these traits, as less independent, less logical, less rational. They saw themselves as stereotypically feminine, "incorporating the negative aspects of femininity...into their self-concepts along with positive feminine aspects."

Some women, of course, do not perceive themselves as lacking in competence; indeed, many women have developed forms of competence usually assigned to males. Their lives, as we see in the next chapter, provide evidence that women can indeed overcome obstacles to competence and freely shape their own choices. But more commonly, adult women today have been told, and go on to tell themselves, that satisfaction and status are to be achieved through the traditional feminine skills--keeping a man happy, managing a home, raising healthy and able children. If this reasonable-sounding theory proves wrong, or holds true only for a short time, they are both puzzled and surprised, and often go on to blame themselves.

Yet before industrialization and over-population reduced the social and economic value of woman's labor in the home and her role in the bearing and rearing of children, traditional feminine competence was in fact a viable means of gaining status, power, and gratification. For certain women in certain situations, indeed the pattern remains so. A moving example of how a special woman in a special time and place found real gratification in the traditional feminine pattern is the psychologist David McClelland's (1975) portrait of his mother-in-law, Grace Waring, who led a rich life centered around sharing and giving. McClelland recalls his earliest acquaintance with the Quaker society from which she came:

> Here were women who gloried in their role, regarding it in no way as a hindrance; yet I could not dismiss them as simple homebodies. As I wondered how this could be, I realized that Quakerism as a religion gives strong support to the sharing rather than the assertive life

> style . . . Everyone is equal before God, and in the silence
> of the Quaker meeting God may speak through anyone,
> male or female . . . The life goal was to develop a certain
> character and to live in a simple, harmonious way rather
> than to achieve a career of great significance (p.
> 108-109).

In such a milieu, concern for others, warmth, and personal generosity were highly prized; developing these qualities enhanced both one's self esteem and one's social value. By embodying these traits Grace Waring won fulfillment on two levels, for herself and in her community as an important and competent person. Such an example, however, is out of the mainstream of American life. The egalitarianism, discouragement of aggression and competition, and the close group ties of the Quakers, mark a religious life without hierarchy or male domination. Opportunities for achieving a sense of competence through such a life style are obviously rare today, despite the attempts of many young people to establish communities with at least some of the characteristics of Quaker life. For most women, during most of their life span, the benefits once inherent in the traditional feminine role must now be derived in other ways.

In the next chapter, we discuss women who have successfully sought out such ways.

Notes

[1]For a different perspective on this pattern, see the discussion of attribution theory in Chapter 7.

II. Successful Women

> If I had a library like yours, all undisturbed for hours, how I would write!...But you see everybody comes to me perpetually. Now this hour since breakfast I have had to decide on the following variety of important questions. Boiled beef -- how long to boil? What perennials will do in Manchester smoke, and what colours our garden wants. Length of skirt for a gown!...See a lady about MS story of hers, and give her heartening but very good advice. Arrange about selling two poor cows for one good one, -- see purchasers, and show myself up to cattle questions, keep, and prices, -- and it's not ½ past 10 yet!
>
> *Letter from Mrs. Gaskell to Eliot Norton, 1857*[1]

Few women are successful, and few successful people are women. In writing this chapter, we were confronted by two difficulties that, we ultimately realized, went to the heart of the problem of successful women. First, in discussing such women, we have often had to explain who they were; their names are simply not that well known. Second, most of the available material concerns the problems rather than the satisfactions of successful women. These difficulties brought home to us what we already knew: that for women, success is still accompanied by such unwelcome baggage as conflict and opposition; and that compared to men, women are less successful.

The present position of women in the occupational structure is documented in data from the 1970 census.[2] Women are still vastly in the minority in most high-status occupations. For example, only 9.2% of physicians, 4.7% of lawyers, 1.6% of engineers, and 28.7% of college and university teachers are women. Most of the women in these fields, moreover, are clustered near the bottom in terms of professional status and financial reward. In 1974, only 5% of persons earning $15,000 or more were women (*New York Times*, December 6, 1976).

These data, of course, speak to the question of women's success, not their competence. Success is defined in the dictionary as the attainment of a desired goal or as the favorable outcome of an undertaking. But success is also socially defined; it implies social recognition, social rewards, social position. Competent people may or may not be successful, in their own eyes or in the opinion of others. Success refers to evaluative judgements made about behavior by the self and others. It often happens, for example, that a writer achieves recognition or "greatness" only many years after death. The reason is not that the writer lacked competence; rather, society did not immediately recognize or value the product of the person's competence. Conversely, one can certainly be successful without being competent, as in the stock illustrations of the executive's son who achieves high position in his father's company although not able to do the job, or of the movie star discovered in an ice-cream parlor whose subsequent fame rests on the competence of the studio's publicity department.

For a competent woman to become successful, many elements must combine. Typically--there are always exceptions--a woman, like a man, needs not only skills or talent but also the personal qualities that enable her to work within her social environment to achieve recognition and position. Society, beginning with parents, must in turn provide a role that is relevant to her competence and must provide the opportunity and mechanisms for learning that role. The fact that there have been more women novelists than women artists, more pianists than conductors, illustrates this point. A writer may learn her trade by reading in the family living room and may practice her craft without publicly trespassing in a male arena. At the other extreme, however, a conductor is not a conductor without an orchestra; and women have not been well received in the role of leader.

There are many points at which our social system has channeled women's competence away from fields in which success brings the highest rewards. At least until recently, many competent women have been barred from medical school; jobs have been unavailable to women lawyers; parents and schools have often discouraged girls from participating in contact sports that might lead to athletic careers. Moreover, sports and play are related to the development of skills important for many roles in later life, as is illustrated by Janet Lever's (1976) analysis of sex differences in the games children play. Conceptualizing peer-group play as a major "agent of socialization," she found that boys and girls differed in the forms of play they engaged in and thus in the skills they acquired. Among the 5th grade children she observed, boys much more often than girls played in large, multi-age groups, and their games were more competitive and longer-lasting than girls. Girls' games typically involved taking turns, as in hopscotch and jumprope. As a consequence, boys more often had to learn how to lead, how to follow, how to subordinate their personal goals to those of the group. Perhaps most important, although rules were complex and thus disputes were frequent, arguments did not disrupt boys' games because they were quick to resolve them. Girls' games were much less likely to require the acquisition of such skills; indeed, quarrels usually resulted in an end to the game.

Many of the interpersonal and organizational skills helpful for success in corporations and other workplaces--coordination of roles, resolution of disagreements--thus remain relatively undeveloped in women. In their book *The Managerial Woman,* Margaret Hennig and Anne Jardim (1977) point out certain consequences of the different experiences men and women bring to their work. Women have difficulty in subordinating their feelings about people to task demands; men have difficulty in interacting with women who join previously all-male groups.

At each step in a woman's career similar obstacles arise, often increasing in intensity and subtlety as the top is approached. Many successful women, therefore, are survivors (or escapees) and their lives deserve our attention.

In this chapter we shall discuss the social and family backgrounds of successful women, the processes by which they became successful, and the problems and satisfactions in their lives, lives which are often valuable models for other women. Similarities and differences in their experiences suggest what changes, both social and personal, might help other women to achieve a more favorable balance of satisfactions to problems.

Certain warnings are necessary, however. First, it has often been the case that to be successful, a woman has had to be unusually competent, especially in relation to men in the same field. While she may thus serve to demonstrate the excellence of which women are capable, an undesirable by-product may be the implication that only the most outstanding women should consider such a field, even though many successful men in the same field do not necessarily possess extraordinary abilities.

Second, because success is in part subjective, a state of mind, one often sees such tragedies as the outstanding male scientist who feels himself a failure because he did not recieve a Nobel Prize. A woman who is a successful scientist is at the present, on the contrary, more likely to be somewhat surprised and pleased by her attainments. It would be unfortunate if women were to become increasingly vulnerable to such irrational feelings of failure.

Backgrounds of Successful Women

Certain characteristics are common in the backgrounds of successful women: being foreign born; having immigrant parents; coming from an affluent family; having one or both parents with high occupational and/or educational status; being an eldest or only child; and having no brothers. These characteristics may occur singly or in combination. Helen Astin (1969), who carried out a large-scale survey of women who had received Ph.D.'s in 1957-58, found that high socioeconomic status and foreign-born parents were more frequent in this group than in the general population, as was the status of eldest or only child. Studies of female political party leaders (Constantini & Craik, 1972) and of women medical students (Cartwright, 1972) have also revealed that such women come from affluent families. According to McDonagh (1975) the same is true of women listed in *Notable American Women*. A study of women mathematicians considered especially creative found that a significantly higher percentage of this select group had either been born outside the United States or had at least one foreign-born parent, compared to less creative women mathematicians or to creative male mathematicians (Helson, 1971). Although eldest-child status distinguished creative male mathematicians, the lack of a brother was what distinguished creative females. In Margaret Hennig's (1970) study of 25 of the then-existing 100 top-level women executives in large companies, not one had a brother, and all were first-born or only children. It appears that when achievement-oriented parents have no boys, a girl, usually the eldest, is sometimes selected as the "son"--the vehicle for parents' achievement wishes and goals.

Willa Cather portrays such a situation in this passage from her novel, *O Pioneers:*

> In his daughter, John Bergson recognized the strength of will, and the simple direct way of thinking things out, that had characterized his father in his better days. He would much rather, of course, have seen this likeness in one of his sons, but it was not a question of choice. As he lay there day after day he had to accept the situation as it was, and to be thankful that there was one among his children to whom he could entrust the future of his family and the possibilities of his hard-won land (1913, p. 24).

Reasons for the advantage of high socioeconomic status seem relatively clear. All other things being equal, in such families money is available for girls' education; and, in addition, parents exemplify and model the values, traits, and goals salient to achievement.[3]

With respect to foreign-born women, those from relatively affluent families often come from societies where wealthy women do neither domestic work nor child care and where they are often expected to have professions or important, if unpaid, positions in aesthetic or charitable activities outside the home. In a symposium on successful women in the sciences sponsored by the New York Academy of Sciences (NYAS), women from various fields reviewed their lives and the forces they perceived as relevant to their success (Kundsin, 1974). For example, Gretchen Minnhaar, an architect from an affluent Argentinian family, pointed out that in her childhood experience, homemaking and child-care activities were traditionally hired out and were not the province of the women of the family. Large numbers of her generation of women entered what are considered in the United States to be traditionally male professions. Only when she came as a young adult to settle in this country, she said, did she realize that "from a mundane architect, I was transformed into a pioneer" (p. 31).

The experience of the immigrant families who are not affluent is quite different. Because the parents are usually strongly motivated to better their position, their children may be explicitly pressured to "make something of themselves" in ways that bring both financial reward and social recognition. Isabelle Karle, a crystallographer, told the NYAS audience of how her Polish-born, immigrant parents taught her reading and arithmetic before she entered school. They urged both her and her brother to become highly educated, suggesting law as well as teaching to her as desirable professions. Karle's mother was a seamstress; although this occupation, like those of many other immigrant women, was of relatively low status, such mothers often had important roles in the family because of their ability to be financial providers and to master the new culture. In this social context, they could serve as competence models for their daughters.

To come from such backgrounds as are described above is clearly not a sufficient guarantee that a girl will be successful; in fact, most girls from such families are not. Moreover, many of the factors we have discussed up to this point--birth order, for example--are out of the control of the women or their families.[4] The ways in which these characteristics affect individuals and the reasons they are associated with success, however, can be analyzed so as to guide decisions and actions that *are* a matter of choice. For example, we have suggested that many foreign-born women are less extensively exposed to harmful sex-role stereotypes, that immigrant families encourage high aspirations, that girls without brothers are likely to become objects of parental achievement drives. Daughters from all families can benefit from such an upbringing.

Economic Motivation

Whether one expects to provide for oneself or expects financial needs to be met by others is a powerful determinant of one's ambitions, goals, decisions, and values. Similarly, parents' beliefs about whether their child will or should become an economic provider affect many aspects of child-rearing. Typically, women have not been brought up to see the role of provider as central to them. Parents often tell daughters that they may have to earn a living, but this is usually in the context of insurance against catastrophe-- failure to find a husband or being deprived of his economic services through illness, death, or divorce. Thus for many girls the earliest impression is that the need to earn a living is associated with stigma and failure, rather than with personal pride or responsibility.

One major exception to this rule is the case of black women. Studies indicate that a majority of black women are raised to expect that they will have to be economic providers (Turner, 1972). Since black men experience serious barriers in their occupational development, mothers of black women are likely to be both models and preachers of the necessity that a girl prepare for supporting a family, rather than expect to be provided for. Such a child may thus be motivated to seek opportunities for achievement. In this way, economic and social forces are reflected in family dynamics. "Role model," "aspirations and expectations," "sex-role socialization"--the very concepts used to explain the absence of success in white women help to explain the pursuit of high occupational status by black women (Epstein, 1973).

A woman who has not been raised to anticipate, accept, or even to value the function of providing for herself or others is in a difficult situation when she is faced with the necessity of doing so. Often her problems rise in proportion to her age at the time. Occasionally, sudden financial need spurs a woman to initiate a career. Susan Groag Bell (1976) in her study of the lives of women in various historical eras who began careers in middle age, found that the threat or actuality of financial disaster did lead some women to employ dormant abilities successfully. Frances Trollope, the 19th-century English novelist and social critic, began her writing career at the age of fifty out of just such financial necessity. No one can count on an undiscovered talent for writing, however, and the woman who realizes in middle age that her talents as well as financial needs would best be served by becoming a physician or a lawyer is in an unenviable situation.

One need not anticipate disaster to endorse the practice of rearing girls to take the responsibility of providing for themselves and for others, to take charge of themselves and their future. Yet most girls experience an *absence* of expectation that they will need to or ought to have lifelong occupations and ought thus to aim as high as possible, and a *lack* of unambivalent praise for their accomplishments. In addition, certain fields of study and certain occupations are made to seem for them unsuitable or unattainable. The needs, goals, and qualities primarily thought to lead to becoming a good wife and mother are the ones that are most encouraged.

In studying successful women, however, we find exceptions to this general picture. When one looks back, or asks them to look back, at their past, quite different themes emerge. These themes concern parents' high aspirations, expectations, and above all encouragement, as well as their support in opposing arbitrary social conventions and sex-stereotyping. The mother often serves as a non-traditional role model for the girl; the father often has a special, close relationship with her and acts as guide, mentor and facilitator. Thus conventional sex-role stereotypes do not take hold, while opportunities for expansion of the personality and for the development of self-confidence are rich.

This description is, of course, somewhat idealized, typical of many successful women, less typical of those who do not attain or pursue success. But many successful women come from less advantageous circumstances. Often they have had at least one parent who was ambivalent, even negative, about their ambitions. Ernesta Drinker Ballard, a horticulturist, said:

> Career aspirations for me, or for my sister, were never mentioned in my family. When at the age of 13, I announced that I wanted be a lawyer, my father smiled and told his acquaintances. But he never took me to his own law office or gave me any idea what the legal profession was all about (Kundsin, 1974, p. 54).

Her career began only in mid-life, and she never did become a lawyer. In Bell's study of nine women who began their careers in mid-life, almost all had mothers who were a negative influence, discouraging their daughter's ambitions, even being a model of what not to become. Although this pattern contrasts sharply with that of such women as the ones studied by Hennig, almost all also had a father or a close male relative who was sympathetic to their aims. Bell suggests that these women were delayed in beginning their careers because of the negative influences of their mothers, while the fact that they had careers at all was usually due to the positive influence of the father or other close male relatives.

Family Influences

A major element in the lives of successful women is the

supportive father. An amazing number and variety of successful women, in accounting for their achievements, have portrayed their fathers as the most influential force in their development.[5] Indeed, Linda Nochlin (1971), in her study of reasons for the rarity of great women artists, found that no woman embarked upon a career as an artist without a male mentor, most often her father, to give her support, encouragement, and access to the "gatekeepers" of the profession. A network of contacts and other practical aids nurtured the career of such artists as Rosa Bonheur, whose father was a drawing master.

Women in other fields have also benefited from their fathers' influence. Margaret Fuller, the American transcendentalist, said of her father, "He hoped to make me the heir of all he knew . . ." (Chevigny, 1976, p. 3). Margaret Sanger, the pioneer of the population-control movement, said shortly before her death, "It was my father more than any other person, who influenced me through his teachings and his vital belief in truth, freedom, right" (J. Reed, 1974). The Nobel laureate in physics, Maria Goeppert-Mayer, was the only child of affluent German parents. Her father encouraged her to have a profession, not to be just a housewife; in fact, as a professor of pediatrics at Göttingen, he preached the importance of permitting children to be adventurous and bold. She told an interviewer that she felt much closer to her father than to her mother because he was more "interesting" (Dash, 1973). The 17th-century scholar, Elena Lucrezia Piscopia, is a dramatic example of the consequences of paternal involvement. Her father "encouraged the development of her brilliant mind because of family pride." She became the first woman Ph.D., receiving a doctorate in philosophy from the University of Padua in 1678. And Eileen McDonagh (1975) found that in a sample of 302 women included in *Notable American Women,* their most important influence was their father.

In a more modern context, Margaret Hennig's studies of women executives (1970, 1977) who had achieved high status in large businesses disclosed a similar pattern; they reported especially close and supportive relationships with their fathers. A variation on the father theme is seen in architect Gretchen Minhaar's reflections on the influences on her life. She singled out her maternal grandfather: "We were the best of friends and traveled together extensively. His sons did not fulfill his dreams of a college degree: I was then a new hope" (Kundsin, 1974). The importance of male support is borne out too by the case of the woman who achieves little until a supportive husband appears on the scene; for example, Mary Somerville, the English 19th-century mathematician, refused a request that she write a book, believing herself incompetent, until her husband persuaded her to do so (Bell, 1976).

The Myth of the Unhappy Childhood

The recurrent theme of family encouragement bears on the question of whether successful women are basically neurotic, compensating for childhood unhappiness, inability to relate to others, and lack of femininity. How powerful is this stereotype is shown by Ravenna Helson (1972), who quotes from a recent book by Edwin Lewis (1968) entitled, ironically, *Developing Women's Potential:*

> The girl who aims for a career is likely to be frustrated and dissatisfied with herself as a person. . . She also probably lacks a close relationship with her family.

Helson then cites, as one of many pieces of evidence to the contrary, a finding that girls with high vocational aspirations were on better terms with their families than those with low aspirations. The business women studied by Hennig overwhelmingly reported warm, close, individual relationships with their parents. Women in medicine (Cartwright, 1972) report a great deal of encouragement from their families. For example, Gertrude Hunter, a pediatrician, recalls that:

> As a woman, I was told, I would be able to do whatever I wanted... This constant, implicit reinforcement of positive self-image was my parents' most valuable gift to me (Kundsin, 1974, p. 58).

Thus, among the variety of advantages experienced by successful women, the most powerful ones appear to be parents (or parental figures) who offer warm encouragement and communicate high aspirations and expectations.[6] From their childhood experiences these women have received an abundance of strength that enables them to survive being perceived as different and deviant, and to work for long periods independently and without encouragement (Anderson, 1974).

Despite these findings, as long as successful women remain few in number, they are by definition atypical, different from the norm. Any person in such a situation risks being stigmatized, isolated, and even ostracized. For most successful women, however, early experiences grant them a degree of immunity to the major danger of all such social pressures: abandonment of one's goal.

Formal Constraints on Women's Occupational Status

All women who pursue careers in high-prestige occupations must cope with at least some of the barriers described in this section; sucessful women are those who have to varying degrees overcome them.

For many women, the first barriers are related to obtaining the training necessary to their careers and to finding suitable positions. Until recently, explicit policies of "no women admitted" were wide spread. Harvard Law School, for example, did not admit women until 1950-51, and for many years after that interviewers from law firms openly stated that they would not hire any women. Patricia Graham (1970), in her account of "Women in Academe," describes a senior professor in a major history department whose remark that "as long as he was a member of the department, there would never be a woman professor in it" was accepted without protest.

Even women who have received their professional education and obtained employment may still face discriminatory rules and regulations. Teachers in public-school systems who became pregnant were often required to leave their jobs after the first trimester. A physicist who was working in industry when she became pregnant recalled that she was immediately laid off: "I wasn't even allowed to enter the laboratory building for three months before the birth to hear a talk or get a book out of my private collection without the special permission of the laboratory director" (Kundsin, 1974, p.46). Although the justification often given for such regulations is that the employer fears a lawsuit if medical complications arise, men are accepted back to work after coronaries and are not laid off if they develop ulcers.

For academic women and some others, regulations against nepotism, prohibiting the employment of husband and wife by the same institution or department, have been major obstacles to personal and professional satisfactions. Joanne Simpson, a meteorologist, stated:

> I believe I have actually suffered more grief and loss of potential productivity form this source than from any other sex-related restriction. I lost my first job (as a university instructor) when I married my first husband (Kundsin, 1974, p. 63).

Such rules are now being fought successfully, in large part because their effect is almost always discriminatory against women.

Even where rules against nepotism are not a problem, a married woman can be adversely affected by the needs of her husband's career. Often she is geographically immobilized, unable and/or unwilling to take the most rewarding job if it means asking a husband to put his career second and go with her, or accept geographical separation. Married congresswomen, for example, report such heroic attempts at a solution as spending a large part of their salaries on commuting expenses, having two households (in their home districts and in the capital) complete with housekeepers, toys, and full refrigerators. The functioning of these legislators is aided by having husbands who are able and willing to move their work to Washington or to accept the separation (*New York Times,* May 24, 1975).

The need for flexible working hours, especially for part-time work, is a major concern for many women, either because they have children or because they expect to have children in the future. One successful woman lawyer was unable to find part-time work in the field of her choice (public service) *even without pay* after her graduation in the 1950's. Although she received the highest marks in her state's bar examination, it was only through the help of the chairman of the Board of Bar Examiners that she found a part-time position.[7] The potential for flexibility is thus a consideration for women in choosing their occupation or specialty. The belief that engineering, medicine, and science require full-time work prevents many young women from choosing these fields (Rossi, 1965). Yet, ironically, it is often in just such fields that flexibility of hours is possible.

Another important group of formalized constraints are social policies, which are made not only by governments but by banks, insurance companies, and other institutions. These rarely are supportive of the woman professional. For example, child-care costs are, at this writing, not fully tax deductible. Women are often ineligible for disability insurance; the presumption is that they are not working out of necessity and will therefore be tempted to drop out by pretending to be ill. Taken together, the underlying message of such policies is that women's careers are not only unimportant but perhaps even undesirable. Changing such discriminatory policies has been an extremely slow process.

Informal Constraints

Some of the most powerful constraints upon women are the stereotypes about them as workers. The most often-heard myth is that, because of family and home responsibility, women tend to be professionally inactive after receiving training.[8] Deans of medical schools frequently have explained on this ground the need to reserve most places for men. Yet many studies have proven that only a minority of professional women drop out for significant periods. Helen Astin (1969) found that 91% of women in her sample were active 7 years after receiving the Ph.D.; in fact, 79% had not interrupted their careers at all, although these women were in their child-bearing years. Many career interruptions in any case occur only because of situations created by employers, such as refusal to permit flexible working hours. And perhaps the fact that women live on the average seven years longer than men can in part be seen as making up for any time taken out for child rearing.

Another stereotype about career women refers to their "neurotic" or aggressive natures. Many women report feeling scrutinized, conspicuous, treated as freaks at work. Since it is always hard to prove a negative, how can anyone prove she is not neurotic, or at least peculiar? Even positive attitudes toward a woman's accomplishment can carry messages of deviance. One lawyer said, "No one seems surprised that my husband has done what he has in life, but my virtually identical career usually causes exclamations of wonder and disbelief'' (A. Reed, 1974). Such attitudes have been described as both ''desexualizing'' and ''deprofessionalizing'' a woman--she is not like other women and she is not like other professionals (Hochschild, 1974). In her discussion of attitudinal barriers to women's occupational advancement, Virginia O'Leary (1974), reviews several studies indicating that men who have the power to decide whether to recommend the promotion of women are often reluctant to do so because of their own unfavorable attitudes about placing women in positions of authority over men. When such a man has a daughter, however, his wish that she not be faced with barriers to her future career may motivate him to support equal opportunities for women in his organization (Kanter, 1977).

Although a successful woman may be seen as unfeminine, at the same time men may consciously or unconsciously choose to handle their problems with such a creature by sexualizing relationships with her. From mild flirtation to direct sexuality, the effect is to diminish a woman's influence and authority. When Margaret Sanger critized a fellow radical, the anarchist editor Alexander Berman, for not supporting her position on birth control, he wrote to her that she was accusing him unjustly: ''Why, if I could only get hold of you dear, you'd have no shadow of doubt about the matter. I'd kiss and hug all your doubts away'' (J. Reed, 1974).

Congresswomen Millicent Fenwick reports that one male colleague, upset by her support for the Equal Rights Amendment, said, ''I just don't like this amendment. I've always thought of women as kissable, cuddly, and smelling good.'' Fenwick promptly responded, ''That's the way I feel about men too. I only hope for your sake that you haven't been disappointed as often as I have'' (*Boston Globe*, May 4, 1975).

Sometimes men's discomfort leads them to avoid women

colleagues. A mathematician remembers that when she enrolled in graduate school, she found on her first day of class that "three seats in front of me, three seats in back of me, and two seats on either side were left vacant." When she joined a faculty, this pattern was at first repeated in department meetings (Kundsin, 1974). Sometimes being included is as painful as being excluded. One lawyer reported, "I was ushered to my first professional meeting, at the Harvard Club in New York, in a freight elevator" (Faircloth, 1974).

A related problem is women's exclusion from the informal networks and mutual support systems that are part of being a powerful, "inside" member of one's profession (Bernard, 1966). These networks and contacts arise not only from colleagues but from old associations with fellow students and former faculty members. the protege system in which older, established professionals become personally involved with and promote the careers of younger colleagues or of students, has usually helped men rather than women. When decisions are made about who gets to hear of a job opening, to present a professional paper, to review a book, being a protege is important. The black woman economist Phyllis Wallace explains her present success as partly due to contacts she made in graduate school:

> A professor of mine got me my first job with a phone call to the National Bureau of Economic Research in New York City. It's through informational ways such as this that you break into the networks. Women and blacks starting out in businesses usually write a letter to personnel and in six months they get an answer saying there is no job. They don't know the informal ball game the way their white male counterparts do (*Boston Globe*, May 26, 1975).

The women executives studied by Margaret Hennig (1970) all succeeded in finding a male mentor, a boss who advised them and acted as buffer and protector. As the boss advanced, they moved up in the company with him.

Women's advancement in male-dominated arenas has further strained the already complex relationships between men and women. Pressures for women to stay out of the world of work often are partly based on a sense that sexual complications arise when men and women work together. In a *Time* magazine article on wives of politicians (October 7, 1974), husbands of several female politicians were also interviewed. One Congresswoman's husband was described as having to "endure inuendoes about the state of his marriage," because his wife was so often seen at public social events with her male associates.

The male ego is the problem here--both the husband's and the employer's. The twin assumptions are that the male ought to be, and psychologically needs to feel, superior. The political husband, according to the same *Time* article on politicians, suffers most from the assumption that his role is a demeaning one. Alice Rossi (1965) found that in the late 1950's, two-thirds of the women she calls "pioneers," those entering male-dominated professions, agreed with the statement, "It is more important for a woman to help her husband's career than to have one herself." A woman physicist recalled the case of a chairman who was reluctant to approach a woman he wanted to hire because her husband might receive a less satisfactory offer and this might precipitate a family crisis. And a recent proposal to place women guards in all-male prisons in Massachusetts was opposed by the union president of guards as well by prisoners on the grounds that "the male ego would never let a woman lock him up" (*Boston Sunday Globe*, November 24, 1974).

In a study of married professional women, described in detail below, Judith Birnbaum (1975) suggests a possible mechanism by which career women who are married resolve conflicts about preserving the male ego. Noticing that they gave unbelievably glorified descriptions of their husbands, she speculated that some women may worry about whether they are truly feminine and by extension whether their husbands are truly masculine. Such a woman may solve this "nasty dilemma" by firmly maintaining the real or fantasy-based conviction that her husband is brilliant and superior and competitively out of her league." Some of the ways these women described their husbands were:

> Knowledge, intelligence, perceptiveness, creativeness, social charm, sensitivity.
> Intellectual prowess, wisdom re people, social charm.
> *He can do anything.* He is kind. He thinks. He is self-possesed and inner-directed.

At the time of this writing, one of high unemployment, there is evidence of a male backlash in reaction to affirmative action and other anti-discrimination programs. In one suburban community, where a federal grant was available for hiring women police trainees in a pilot study of the feasibility of integrating women into police departments, a man on the Civil Service List, who had spent over three years wating for a job opening, said in a newspaper interview, "I've been discriminated against for years. First it was blacks, then Puerto Ricans. Now it's women" (*Boston Globe*, February 17, 1975). Whether or not his perception of discrimination is accurate, there is an inhibiting effect upon women from the anger of men around them. Given the lack of social suport for the ambitions of women, strong negative feedback from men can be a powerful dissuader, particularly for women at transitional points in their lives: a mature woman returning to work or considering a promotion or a young girl deciding about future career goals.[9]

Successful Women as Mothers

Special constraints affect successful women who are also mothers. Many employers are skeptical about hiring women with children, and openly express the belief that they must be either unreliable as workers or inferior as mothers. Married women with children in fact have heavy drains on their time and energy; yet they are the most vulnerable to the "pressure for competence in a range of roles" that is demanded of all career women (Epstein, 1974). Mothers' opportunities to cook gourmet meals, sew fancy costumes, and especially to shape young minds is infinite. Mothers are also likely to receive, and to be vulnerable to, negative messages about their career commitments. Few feel immune from criticism about being away from their children or being busy, tired, preoccupied.

For them, single-minded, conflict-free concentration on professional concerns is almost impossible, for the needs of others are consistently in their consciousness.

Much of the gratification girls receive from achievement, as Lois Hoffman (1972) points out, traditionally derives from gaining the approval of others. But the praise so easily elicited from parents by a young girl's winning a spelling bee (or even a science competition) in the early school years, is rarely forthcoming when as a mother she wins a prize requiring travel to address a professional meeting.

Thus the price of success is greater for women with children, not only that, but it may increase with increasing success. Conflicts of needs and priorities that cause anguish to women do in fact exist when the person in a high position is also the mother of young children. One such woman, a lawyer teaching at a major law school, says:

> To be sitting in a committee meeting (that easily could have been adjourned half an hour before), and to be worried about getting home to your child who may be

hungry or lonely, is something few men ever have to
think about (Meacham, 1974).

The reader will recall the letter by the novelist Mrs. Gaskell
quoted at the beginning of this chapter which reveals not only
the numerous demands on her but her own need and wish not
to cheat her family because of her work. Other letters con-
firm this attitude:

> I like to keep myself in readiness to give [my family]
> sympathy or advice at any moment; and consequently
> do not, as I am tempted to do, shut myself up secure
> from any interruption.
>   When I had *little* children I do not think I could have
> written stories because I should have become too much
> absorbed in my fictitious people to attend to my real
> ones (Quoted in Bell, 1976).

Mrs. Gaskell appears to exemplify the syndrome of
"supermom" described by Madeline Bedell (1973). This syndrome arose as a way of mitigating guilt about working,
which, women were told, "just might be all right, provided
we did not neglect children, husband, and home." To let a
husband help would undermine supermom's need to preserve
his "male prerogative"; to let the children help would set
them apart from the more fortunate children of non-working
mothers.

The woman who frees herself from the belief that she must
shoulder most of the responsibilities of family life still faces
the question of how to reduce them to a manageable quanti-
ty. Obviously she needs assistance with care of children and
home. Such possible sources as husbands, daycare centers,
and professional housecleaning services of course should
become more widely available and acceptable. When it comes
to more subtle responsibilities, however, such as attending to
the needs of elderly parents or meeting the special demands of
holidays and house guests, these tend to remain the province

of the woman, who, if she has a truly demanding job, too often still must choose between guilt and exhaustion in deciding how to deal with them.

Barriers to Advancement

The socialization of girls does not typically prepare them to move comfortably into professional roles. Incongruity and inconsistency exist between traits and behaviors associated with traditional femininity and those important for professional advancement. In work situations where highly placed women are rare, the absence of role models or social supports makes it hard for a woman to know how to handle herself; non-productive and defensive reactions often result. Within most prestigious professions or occupations, women are indeed a minority, often present in such small numbers as to be virtually alone among men. Under such circumstances, studies indicate, any token person, including a woman, no matter how she acts, is seen as special and different, if only because she is a novelty; psychological research on cognition and perception has shown that a novel stimulus elicits disproportionate attention (Taylor & Fiske, 1976).

Because women often feel conspicuous, and beyond that criticized, they may behave in ways that impede their advancement. Those in high positions, for instance, must learn to mobilize and utilize the assistance of others; yet one business executive confessed her difficulty in delegating tasks: "The men who work for me always think I can't do the job if I give it to them, and people don't accept being told by a woman, so I end up doing it myself" (*The New York Times,* February 5, 1975). Women have been more likely than men to have problems in this area, perhaps because delegating authority is not part of the feminine role. The role of housewife and mother is actually the direct opposite; it consists in large part of doing precisely those things that others are unable or unwilling to do for themselves.

As a reaction to this conflict of role, successful women sometimes adopt a posture of superfemininity. In the NYAS symposium (Kundsin, 1974), several women made such statements as "In my work I wear tailored clothing, but always very feminine" (p. 30). Another woman took pains to mention that her daughters were "accomplished seamstresses, cooks, and home decorators" (p. 34). The 19th century artist Rosa Bonheur felt impelled to justify wearing trousers by the exigencies of her work, her need to be close to horses in order to study them:

> Despite my metamorphoses of costume, there is not a daughter of Eve who appreciates the niceties more than I do; my brusque and even slightly unsociable nature has never prevented my heart from remaining completely feminine (Nochlin, 1971).

Relationships with other women constitute a problem for some successful women. Feminists and anti-feminists alike have noted an absence of strong bonds among women. In interviewing women lawyers, Cynthia Epstein (1971a) found that they tended to criticize each other as unstable, difficult, or unfeminine. In a study of women managers, 90% believed that other women were more competitive and jealous toward them than were men. One woman attributed this to the fact that "Women don't play stickball when they're kids. They haven't learned teams" (*New York Times*, February 5, 1975). One must recognize here that women's status in society is inferior to men's, and that they live in relative isolation from each other, but in intimate contact with members of the dominant group. In such situations, women, like members of minority groups, are vulnerable to identifying with dominant (male) attitudes toward women, denigrating other women in an attempt to maintain their self-esteem. Some may therefore need to learn the rewards of identifying with other women and working cooperatively.

The "queen bee" syndrome (Staines, Tavris, & Jayaratane, 1974) is an interesting variation on this theme. Some women who have been succesful within the present system value their special status and do not want competition from other women. Hence they tend to deny that discrimination exists, believing that any woman who is able and determined enough can "make it"; explicitly or implicitly they see those who have not made it as inferior. A commentator on the NYAS talks (Kundsin, 1974) made this point: many of the speakers made statements reflecting a need to deny discrimination and to minimize any special problems associated with being a woman. Though they claimed they had encountered little prejudice or hardship because of their sex, they also told stories of indifference from a thesis advisor, inability to seek a more satisfying job because of a husband's work, forced separation from a child during professional training, discouragement by guidance counselors. Their denials of discrimination seemed to arise out of something other than the facts.

Rosabeth Kanter (1977), in her study of organizations and women, has concluded that three structural factors explain much of women's behavior and difficulties: their lack of opportunity for advancement; their low power; and their status as tokens or as a minority. Given these components, she points out, one can predict how any person will behave, male or female, white or black. Men who see no chance for advancement in their work are as unlikely to express high aspirations as are women. Thus psychological explanations that ignore structural factors may fail to address (and correct) important determinants of women's work-related problems.

Implications for Change

What changes must we have for women to become more successful, and for more women to become successful?

Structural aspects of occupations obviously come high on the list. Flexibility of working hours, for men as well as for women, can provide relief from the juggling act women must perform when they have family responsibilities (Stein, Cohen & Gaden, 1976). Such flexibility might include: granting full professional status to part-time workers who otherwise meet all requirements; exploring the use of the four-day week (Poor, 1970); allowing choices about when one begins the day; permitting two people to share jobs. Newspapers have reported sharing by husbands and wives in such diverse occupations as the ministry and truck driving.

Also important are reforms in the area of fringe benefits-- sickness, absences, leaves. Many women must pretend that they themselves have the flu, when actually it is their child who has chicken pox. Permitting individuals to decide what use to make of their sick leaves can humanize work with no loss of productivity.

Maternity leave is still an explosive topic; it raises such emotion-laden issues as the desirability of child-bearing given the population explosion, and the responsibility of parents versus society for the burdens of children. Patricia Graham (1970) suggests that for colleges and universities to grant leave with pay for up to two childbirths would, over the life of a woman at the institution, be a reasonable cost to pay for making the conditions of her career more humane. The granting of paternity leaves also increases the options of professional parents. At present, however, many professional women must face a multititude of questions: whether, and how, to have their babies at a slow time--in the summer, for academics; whether to go back to work in the shortest possible time regardless of personal preference, often because there is no paid maternity leave; whether to lose professional ground by temporarily decreasing their career commitments.

Because of the present likelihood that a woman in a male-dominated occupation will be surrounded by men in her work situation, another change becomes obvious. Men need to recognize their discomfort with women colleagues, to discuss it openly, and to understand that the way to reduce it, both for themselves and for women, is not to exclude women but to admit more as colleagues.

In some fields, it is encouraging to note, the near future can be expected to bring rapid changes in the proportions of males and females. Over 30% of the entering classes of many major medical schools, for instance, are now women. Even such conservative institutions as churches and the armed forces have gradually been removing restrictions on the roles permitted to women.

Is It Worth It?

In this chapter we have inevitably focused on the strains and conflicts experienced by successful women. The cumulative picture is of struggle, the painful reality of which is recognized by the scientist Joanne Simpson in her response to the question of whether her own struggle has been worth-while:

> Right now it does not appear to me that either the scientific contribution, the position I have reached, or the rewards are enough to compensate for the terrible price extracted from me and from those close to me (Kundsin, 1974, p. 66).

Is this the experience of most successful women? Objective evidence about rewards and costs is rare, for few studies focus on this point. The most relevant is that carried out by Judith Birnbaum (1975), who compared three groups of able women in midlife: single professional women; married professionals with children; and homemakers who had not worked since the birth of their first child. Both single and married professional women had higher levels of satisfaction and self-esteem and saw themselves as more competent than did the homemakers. The homemakers also felt less atractive than did the married professionals. Most of the women Birnbaum studied however, were in their forties, a time when the more severe struggles professional women experience may be passed. Homemakers, in contrast, at this stage of their lives may be facing increased stress over the growing independence of their children. For either men or women, there is no way of life that will be consistently rewarding and tension-free. There is no basis, therefore, on which to preach to women about what their pattern should be; one can only warn that all patterns contain both the risk of disappointments and the promise of deeply rewarding experiences.

There is reason to hope that the rewards will increasingly prevail for those who choose to be committed to careers. It has always been the case that some women have experienced enormous gratifications from such a pattern. In her history of women's struggle for full membership in the medical profession, Mary Roth Walsh (1977) describes the sentiments of Harriot Hunt, a pioneer nineteenth-century physician. Despite ostracism by male colleagues (who wondered "if she knew the sternum from the spinal column"), she summed up her life to a younger physician: "I have been so happy in my work; every moment is occupied; how I long to whisper it in the ear of every listless woman, 'do something if you would be happy'."

Notes

[1] Quoted by Susan Groag Bell, (1976).

[2] Women's Bureau, United States Department of Labor, *Detailed occupations of employed professional and technical workers, by sex, 1970.*

[3] For a discussion of the relationship of social class to achievement, see Rosen, (1956).

[4] Feminists are concerned about the likelihood that one *will* soon be able to choose the sex of a child (Keith-Speigel, Fidell, & Hoffman, 1974): since this is predicted to increase the number of two-child families of boy first, girl second, fewer girls will be in the position most often associated with achievement.

[5] One must weigh carefully the evidence for the importance of the father. Because of the relative scarcity of women achievers, the usual research strategy has been to identify a sample of already successful women and try to figure out what has made them that way. One needs to remember that such studies, like autobiographies, rely on a recall of the past that tends to be selective and imperfect. In addition, many such studies used no control groups. It may be, therefore, that in a sample of women who are not "successful" one would find evidence for similar closeness to the father. Finally, because successful women are so rare, generalization from their experiences to women in general is risky; from what we know about successful women, we can only make tentative suggestions about how fathers can nurture girls' competence.

[6] Such a pattern is also found in male achievers, as is demonstrated in Rosen and D'Andrade (1959).

[7] This account is taken from the February 1974 issue of the *Harvard Law School Bulletin,* which deals with women lawyers.

[8] The life experiences of almost all successful women have been affected by the social norm that women are expected to marry and have children. Therefore, the issues discussed in this section are often as relevant to single as to married women.

[9] Women also report being dissuaded by negative feedback from other women.

III. Father and Daughters

Clap hands, clap hands
Till father comes home;
For father's got money,
But mother's got none.

Becoming the father of a daughter brings with it many opportunities and some confusion.[1] The increasing variety of options for women--about careers, marriage, children--entails increased ambiguities; a father may no longer have any clear notion of what his daughter's life will be as an adult. Yet in thinking about the part he wishes to play in her upbringing and the ways to have a beneficial effect on her growth, he must develop just such a vision of her future life, which then becomes the basis for the kind of father-daughter relationship he may seek to create.

We believe that girls need to acquire such forms of competence as will give them the most choices in later life, and that fathers can have a crucial impact on the development of their daughter's competence. In this chapter we shall discuss such questions as: How are father-daughter relationships affected by cultural and social forces? How are the traditional images of fatherhood changing? Which of the many ways to be a "good" father are most promising in fostering a daughter's competence?

Traditional Views of the Father

It is only recently that fathers have received attention in the child development literature, either popular or scientific. In many previous works on child psychology, even major works, "father" was not even an entry in the index (Nash, 1965). An exception to this past neglect is the psychoanalytic literature, but here, in both clinical and theoretical papers, the father is considered mainly in terms of his effect upon his daughter's erotic development and upon her future ability to have satisfying heterosexual relationships. In these terms the proof of his adequacy as a father rests upon the success of her marriage. While this aspect of the father's role is important, it covers only a part of the contribution he can make to her development. In fact, as we shall see, too much focus on this theme has had undesirable consequences.

With the onset of World War II and its impact upon the family, fathers began to be noticed, but mainly by virture of their absence. When researchers began to study the effects of a father's absence, early findings in studies of both sons and daughters seemed to indicate that the absence posed more problems for sons (Biller, 1971, 1974; Biller & Weiss, 1970). Possibly the sparseness of results for daughters lay in the fact that in 58 of 60 major studies the effects on daughters were not the primary focus (Herzog & Sudia, 1974). Researchers obviously assumed that the father's most important interactions were with his son. Recently, however, in a study of adolescent daughters of widowed and divorced mothers, possible delayed effects of father absence were explored by comparing these girls with others from intact families. The researcher, E. Mavis Hetherington (1972), reasoned that since young girls without fathers would be most affected in future relationships with males, these problems would become obvious after puberty, when involvement with the opposite sex became salient. Using the technique of actually observing the behavior of adolescent girls with a male interviewer, she did find certain deviant patterns associated with a father's absence; the patterns differed, moreover, according to whether death or divorce caused the absence. Daughters of divorcees sought closeness and attention from their interviewer to an inappropriate degree; daughters of widows were overly inhibited and restrained. In several ways, however, these girls may not have been typical of girls who had lost their fathers. First, their mothers had not remarried; second, they were from the working class, where the effects of a depressed income such as almost always accompanies a father's absence are particularly severe. For such reasons, their mothers may have been poorly equipped to carry on successfully alone.

The major concerns of such studies of paternal absence have been with the adequacy of children's personality adjustments and their deviations from normal sex-role development. Perhaps because competence in women has been neither highly valued nor viewed as crucial to mental health, effects upon daughters' competence were not examined--even though studies of competent women make clear the major role their fathers have played in their development.

The Father-Child Relationship: Its Nature and Importance

With attention newly focused on the father's role, debate

rages about the nature, function, and ideal degree of involvement of fathers in child care (Beels, 1974; Biller & Meredith,
1974; Lamb, 1976b). Such issues must be viewed in the context of the economic and social structure of a particular society; they are deeply embedded in the nature of family roles and
the division of labor between men and women. Most
Americans have either lived within or aspired to a family
model that we will call traditional, consisting of a married
couple and their unmarried children, living together in a
separate household. In this model, the man has the functional
or instrumental role of sole financial supporter, or breadwinner (Parsons, 1955). Usually he works away from the
household, leaving the wife to take on most of the household
and child-care tasks and to deal with the emotional needs of
the family; the father's energies must be preserved for his encounters with the outside world.

When the father functions thus primarily as an "absent"
worker, several often unnoticed consequences ensue.
Although the household schedule revolves around his needs,
he is not expected to contribute much labor to household
tasks. He is a novelty, almost an honored guest. Susan Ford
recalls that, before her father became President, he "really
just wasn't home a lot, so when he was there, it was so special
we did everything we could to make him happy--and he did
everything he could to make us happy" (*Time,* October, 17,
1974).

The wife and children clearly are supporting players in this
scenario. Such major decisions as whether the family shall
move depend upon the career of the father. More important,
in such traditional families the daughter's future role is also
seen in traditional terms; her father is not likely to have much
concern for, or give high priority to, developing her competence, much less preparing her for a career. Rather, such
qualities as being warm and loving, being attractive and eager
to please, and attending to the needs of others, including her

father, seem more important to the family. Even the busy father who feels little direct responsibility for child care probably is concerned to foster independence and achievement in his son; but his daughter he may view as someone he can simply relax with and enjoy. In his recent book "How to Father", psychologist Fitzhugh Dodson (1974) advises fathers about "some of the general things that a father may spend time doing [with a] boy. First, he can take him along when he needs to by something at a hardware store or sporting goods store. He can teach him some of the basic skills such as catching or throwing a football or baseball...He can take him to spectator sports such as baseball, football, soccer...He can take him hiking,camping, or fishing." Dodson then seeks to reassure the many fathers who are "at a loss" as to what to do with a daughter: "You can take her out to lunch, which will be a special treat and a valued experience... Fathers forget they are the model for the kind of husband [their daughter] will be looking for in later life. That's why a warm relationship with father is valuable for a girl, however it is expressed (p. 213-214).

To many researchers, indeed, it is an important function of the father, more than of the mother, to differentiate clearly the male and female roles for his sons and daughters by having different expectations and making different demands for them (Johnson, 1963). Many "experts" still endorse this function, with no question about the consequences for girls.

One such expert is the prominent pediatrician T. Berry Brazleton, who sees the traditional model as one of "awareness of a firmly established, different role for each parent." A man's work life, he argues, should not be seen as competitive with his family life but as "the very core of his position in the family." His absence should be viewed by the wife as a sign of his devotion and should be described as such to the children. Children will feel cheated by the brevity of their time with their father "only if Mother 'feels sorry' for the child because Daddy comes home late..." (Brazleton, 1970).

It follows from this model that the father who is willing to sacrifice occupational status in order to have more time for his family is looked on as deficient in manliness. Few would argue that a father's presence and involvement in family life are wrong or pathological; in fact, in our society it is important psychologically for men to establish their manliness by having children. Yet ironically the next step, being caring and nurturant toward their children, raises questions about manliness. Men who seek a lifestyle facilitating involvement with their families are often suspected of being escapists, anxious over competition and unsure of their abilities.

That fathers are not biologically programmed to feel strong attachments to their children is another argument, based on findings of biologists and anthropologists. The biologist Robert L. Trivers (1972) has suggested that under many circumstances, from the evolutionary perspective of maximizing the number of one's offspring, the best male strategy (and one likely to be favored by natural selection) would be to remain relatively uninvolved in child care and to have more than one sexual partner. David Gutmann (1973) has suggested that male concern for children is fragile; men direct their potentially violent aggression away from children only in a social structure where they are the economic providers and believe themselves to be the dominant sex.

The new wave of researchers studying the father's role, especially those concerned with father-infant relationships (Pedersen & Robson, 1969), offers a different viewpoint. A natural father-child bond does exist, they argue, but is weakened by the traditional father role, in which, for example, the father is away from home for long periods of time (Lynn, 1974). Typically, fathers have only a brief period with their children in the morning and perhaps barely an hour with them before bedtime (Kotelchuck,1972). Yet the phenomenon of engrossment--the heightened self-esteem and absorption observed in men when they first meet their newborns-- provides evidence of a strong and natural father-child bond. Investigators believe that this reaction is adaptive for survival and probably innate, but that it has been interfered with by such hospital practices as restricting physical contact with in- fants (Greenberg & Norris, 1974).

Relevant here is Margaret Mead's description of her husband's first encounter with their daughter, Cathy:

> Gregory came home from England when she was six weeks old. We let the nurse go and took care of her ourselves for a whole weekend during which she had a bad episode of colic. This was the only time he took much physical care of her. But it was enough to establish a very close relationship between Gregory and Cathy...There is something in the kind of response a very young baby evokes, perhaps with its hand that still retains the infantile grasping reflex and curls so firmly and trustfully around an adult finger, that brings the father in and wins his enthusiasm. If this close contact is postponed--if the father believes that a baby must be ap- proached gingerly or must be kept at arm's length--his relationship to his child will be drastically different from the mother's, and the experience of children of the two sexes also will be forever different (1972, p. 263).

The psychologist Milton Kotelchuck (1972), tested the assumption that infants' ties to their mothers are stronger than their attachments to their fathers. Using a standard research situation in which one-year old children (white, middle-class) in an experimental room were exposed to the entrances and departures of mothers, fathers, and strangers, he compared reactions to mothers' and fathers' departures by observing such behaviors as crying and the cessation of play.

The children reacted, he found, with as much protest and distress to the departure of their fathers as their mothers, much less strongly to the departure of the stranger. The behavior of boys and girls was similar. By interviews he found that the average amount of time per day fathers played with their children was significantly longer for sons than for daughters; on the average fathers played an hour with their daughters, about 1.7 hours with their sons.

These experiments were repeated in Guatemala with peasant children, who proved to be more upset by the departures of their mothers than of their fathers. A major reason, according to the investigators, may be that Guatemalan fathers take part even less in the care of their young children than do American fathers (Lester, Kotelchuck, Spelke, Sellers, & Klein, 1974).

The evidence of a strong father-child bond presented by Kotelchuck's studies is supported by the research of Michael Lamb, whose longitudinal studies of fathers and infants were based upon home visits rather than observations in a laboratory (Lamb, 1976a). When the children were seven to eight months old, an age at which child development theory predicts the peak of anxiety reactions to strangers and attachment to the mother, Lamb found that, on most measures of attachment, the babies preferred their fathers. For such critical attachment behaviors as being held and being comforted when distressed, they showed an equal attachment to both parents. The babies seemed more playful in their interactions with their fathers, Lamb noticed, and found this to be related to the fathers' own playfulness; play, he thought, might be a special component of father-infant relationships. Given the adaptive quality of play as a vehicle for learning to master the environment, one may even deduce a kind of survival value for infants in their interactions with their fathers. In our culture, fathers may need some encouragement and guidance to facilitate their engagement in such activities. Just as in the occupational world women are helped by male mentors, Robert Fein (1973) suggests, wives may serve as female mentors with respect to their husbands' acquisition of competence in child care. And the fact that fathers can and do carry on as single parents (Levine, 1976) highlights the unused capacities many fathers have for being complete parents.

How Fathers View Daughters

A man's feelings and beliefs about having a girl-child exist well before her birth. Such attitudes as those of the actor Richard Burton are widely shared, although rarely so fancifully implemented:

> Just before he proposed to Princess Elizabeth of Yugoslavia, he gave an English magazine a handwritten advertisement for a woman under 38 to bear him a child for a fee. Explained the actor: "The sound of a little son running around again would be the saving of me." The price offered, however, was...$50,000 for a boy, $25,000 for a girl (*Time,* November 25, 1974).

Most men (and women) strongly prefer to have a boy, studies show, especially for their first or only child (Dinitz, Dynes, & Clarke, 1954; Westoff & Rindfuss, 1974). A recent study of the "family interactive system" of infants, mothers, and fathers, found interesting and significant patterns in families of male infants but not of females. The researcher, speculating on the reason for this difference, noted that when asked during pregnancy about which sex they preferred, every parent wanted a boy. The birth of a girl apparently brought on for the parents a period of distress and disequilibrium that overshadowed other influences (Pedersen, 1975). Often then, a man whose wife has just given birth to a baby girl may, for reasons he cannot fully identify, feel disappointed, deprived, or even ashamed.[2]

Many explanations have been offered for the almost universal desire for male offspring. Before looking at its deeply rooted cultural reasons, let us allow fathers themselves to explain it. The two most frequent reasons fathers gave in one study for wanting a son were the desire to perpetuate the family name and the belief that they could understand a boy more easily than a girl. Other reasons included being better able to identify with the child, and having too many women in one's life already! Although mothers greatly preferred to have a boy as their firstborn, the only frequently expressed reason was that their husbands wanted a son (Goodenough, 1957).

Our belief is that the underlying reason for a male child's desirability is the universally higher status of the male sex. The desire is especially strong in patrilineal societies, where ancestry is traced through the father and property is handed down through male heirs. Many parts of the Old Testament exhibit deep concern about maintaining and ensuring the continuity of the family, a concern reflected in the laws of inheritance, which permitted property to be handed down only from father to son. Exceptions did not affect this basic structure. When a man had no sons, daughters were permitted to inherit property but had to pass it on to their own sons (Bird, 1974).

Much of this tradition still persists, strengthened by the human desire to create a tangible legacy that will endure after death. While in societies such as our own, women can arrange to acquire property and transmit it to their children, they have so far rarely taken such steps; few, after all, purchase life-insurance policies. This situation follows of course from the tendency for men to be, or to be perceived as, the major economic providers.

The prospect of a first child still creates in most men the desire for a male heir to assure their place in society both present and future. In Jewish culture, the birth of a son confers special status on the father because of the dominant role of the male in religious life; only a male, for instance, can say the special prayers for the dead. A ceremonial circumcision (or *bris*) marks the boy's entry into the Jewish community, which is essentially a community of males; the mother is not present at the ceremony. The birth of a female child is not an occasion for similar ceremony and rejoicing.[3]

Although male preference is almost universal,[4] some men do prefer daughters. Two researchers recently explored such cases. Robert Fein (1973) studied men before and after the birth of their first child. The men interviewed, although heterogeneous in occupation, were mostly middle-class and were perhaps somewhat atypical in that they all attended childbirth preparation classes with their wives. Several were in professions related to the behavioral sciences. Of the thirty men interviewed, eight expressed a desire for a girl. Four of these gave reasons that mainly reflected concern or self-doubt about their ability to do a good job of rearing a son--for example, because of a difficult relationship with their own fathers. The others had positive reasons for wanting girls--an interest in feminism, the belief that their wife would be an excellent model for a girl, the opinion that being a firstborn would counteract the difficulties of being a girl in this society, and the feeling that having had a fine relationship with their mother, they would do unusually well in relating to a daughter. The wives of these men, it is interesting to note, were more likely than wives of other subjects to be deeply involved in careers and to plan an early return to work after the birth of a baby. Thus there may be some link between a man's participating in an egalitarian relationship in which his wife has a serious career commitment and his being eager or willing to have a firstborn girl.

David Gangsei (1974) interviewed eight men who were expecting their first child. Several wanted girls for quite idiosyncratic reasons. One couple anticipated so much fuss and family involvement if they had a boy (because they were Jewish and would be pressured to have a *bris*) that it seemed less complicated to have a girl. One man who was eager to have a girl pictured her as a daddy's girl, constantly adoring him. Another man, who had wanted a boy but had a girl, adapted to the situation by similar fantasies of a worshipful daughter running to him as he came home from work.

After a child is born, its sex profoundly affects how the father sees his child. Fathers of newborn daughters, compared with those of newborn sons, according to one study, were more likely to perceive their babies as delicate, weak, soft, fine-featured, even though the investigators had established by various measurements that no actual differences in these traits existed between the male and female babies (Rubin, Provenzano, & Luria, 1974). It is only a step from perceiving one's daughter as weak and soft to apprehension about her fragility and need for protection. Indeed, several studies report that fathers participate in more rough-and-tumble play with their sons and in more "care-taking" activities with their daughters (Tasch, 1952).

In a more general way, the expectations of fathers for their sons and daughters as adults surely affect the values, attitudes, and behaviors they exhibit toward their children. At least until recently, the future envisioned by fathers for their daughters rarely included serious work, while such a vision was central to the expectations for their sons.

In an interview study with middle-class fathers of preschool-age girls and boys, Aberle and Naegele (1952) found that the greatest sex-related differences were in parental attitudes toward educational attainment. Fathers were far more likely to expect their child to go to college if that child was a son rather than a daughter. Findings from our own recent research (Barnett & Baruch, 1977) suggest that this difference in expectations may no longer exist. Fathers, as well as mothers, of preschool-age girls place as high a value as do fathers and mothers of preschool-age boys on the child's completing a college education and earning her or his own living. One interpretation of these data is that since today's parents envision for their daughters a future in which they will be economic providers, they believe the girls should therefore be reared to pursue occupational achievement.

A reality of having a daughter is that she is a member of the opposite sex. Therefore, a major theme to be aware of in father-daughter relationships is the sexual; a theme not always acknowledged, but clearly apparent in a study of two- to four-year-old boys and girls whose parents were interviewed about masculine and feminine traits in their children. Fathers often mentioned coquetry as the mark of their daughters' femininity, and one father frankly remarked, "Femininity can't be divorced in my mind from a certain amount of sexuality"(Goodenough, 1957).

Historically, female sexuality has, of course, aroused ambivalent emotions in males (McLaughlin, 1974). Biblical and medieval theology texts yield many references to woman as seductress, temptress, harlot, adultress; and the restrictions on women found in various cultures often are intended to protect males (and the females belonging to them) from sexual temptation. Such texts also, however, portray women as innocent, pure, virginal.

Warnings to young girls about the sexual dangers associated with males more than likely influence how they respond to their fathers. There is evidence for the pervasiveness of concern about sexuality in such diverse forms as strict rules governing male teachers' relations to female students in high schools, the practice of having a female nurse present at gynecological examinations by male physicians, and other taboos around touching, taboos stricter for men than for women.[5]

When sexual themes emerge in father-daughter relationships, they are usually accompanied by feelings of distress and shock. A mother recently wrote an anonymous account in a popular women's magazine of the problems arising from the precocious puberty of her eight-and-one-half-year-old daughter, Melissa (*Family Circle,* August, 1974). In addition to Melissa's anxiety about developing breasts and about other physical changes, she began to feel that ther father was angry at her. He no longer picked her up and hugged her when he came home from work, and he stopped playing a favorite "tickle" game at bedtime. When her mother asked the father about it, she was shocked by his response:

> Don't you see that I can't think of her as my little girl, the way I used to? I know it doesn't make sense but there's something inside of me that says she's on her way to growing up, that I have to treat her differently. Look, it's crazy, but when I hug her or roughhouse with her, I'm afraid of accidentally touching her..."

His fears are echoed in the words of such professionals as the psychiatrist Marjorie Leonard (1966):

> It takes a mature man, one who has found an unneurotic solution to his own Oedipal conflict and has achieved a satisfying marriage relationship, to be able to offer his daughter desexualized affection at the crucial stages in her development.

Such a view would eliminate all divorced men from the ranks of good fathers. And who can be sure he has resolved his Oedipal conflicts, which, we all know, are mostly unconscious? Such warnings, whatever their validity, may intimidate men and make them self-conscious in their relationships with their daughters, thus interfering with easy and natural companionship. And yet one cannot deny the presence of sexuality in these relationships and the resulting anxiety.

During adolescence many girls experience a sense of estrangement. Thus an often mutual withdrawal occurs, unfortunately, at a time when a girl could most benefit from sharing and closeness. The father's inhibitions, moreover, must be seen in the context of social attitudes that prescribe discouragement of tenderness, physical contact, and emotionality in males (Feigen-Fasteau, 1974), inhibitions learned early and well. Michael Lewis and his associates (Lewis, Weinraub & Ban, 1972), studying early development of boys and girls and the way each is treated by fathers and mothers, point out that behavior patterns such as touching and hugging (proximal) are permitted to girls and are more characteristic of them than of boys; the latter are encouraged early and vigorously to use such non-physical modes as talking and looking. In later life, fathers and sons share this socialization bias, while mothers and daughters remain freer to express closeness. A father and a daughter, therefore, must seek ways of overcoming these barriers to feeling.

Some mothers may feel threatened by too strong an attachment of daughters and fathers; this too affects father-daughter relationships. The theme of mother-daughter competition for the father is a familiar, perhaps even an overstated one; but when a mother feels inadequate and disappointed, or has a personal history sensitizing her to rivalry, it can become powerful. While a man may at first feel some enjoyment at being the object of intense interest to two females, he may soon sense danger and react by lessening his involvement with his daughter.

How Daughters View Fathers

From a daughter's point of view, what shapes her relationship to her father? For one thing, the lower status of women in our society. Because children learn about themselves and their relations to others by watching their parents, and because the attitudes of their parents, in turn, are shaped by the culture, girls know from an early age where women stand in our society. And not surprisingly, girls express the desire to be a boy far more often than boys for being a girl (Brown, 1958). When asked, girls say often they would like to grow up to be a daddy; one rarely hears a boy express interest in becoming a mommy. Such feelings persist as girls grow older.

These attitudes have been acknowledged for years by psychoanalysts, who have, however, ascribed them to penis envy, that is, feelings of jealousy, rivalry, and inadequacy generated by the girl's sense of anatomical deficiency. We do not question the existence of such feelings in young girls; their intensity and duration, however, will vary with the particular social structure, with the degree of imbalance of power and the role division in a girl's own home. While these are greater in a traditional family, the girl from even the most liberated household cannot escape awareness of cultural values that grant higher status and greater importance to that which is male.

In two studies separated by more than fifteen years, young girls were found to perceive fathers as the parent who was strong, smart, and the boss; mothers as the parent who was friendly and nurturant, taking care of the house and the children (Baruch & Barnett, 1977; Kagan & Lemkin, 1960). Girls also saw the father as the one who earned money. In our own study, which focused on white, middle-class preschoolers, we were able to examine the relationship of the girls' images to what was actually happening in the family. We found that whether the mother worked made no difference in the concepts these girls had of their parents. What did matter was the extent to which fathers performed child-care tasks, such as cleaning the child's room, taking her to school, supervising her morning routine. It was important, moreover, that he perform these tasks independently rather than jointly with his wife. The more he did so, the less likely his daughter was to have stereotyped images of her parents. Thus fathers who participate in the care of their daughters are also helping to prevent and/or undo stereotypic attitudes.

Few fathers yet participate fully in child care, however, and most girls still perceive fathers as the dominant parent. Too often, under such circumstances, the daughter may grow either to feel resentful and rebellious both toward her father and toward men in general, or to acquiesce, adopting an adoring, passive, subservient posture. A girl's choice of either reaction is not consciously planned but is influenced by many interacting factors. These include her personality and even her physical appearance--whether she is petite and delicate looking; the example her mother sets; the kind of man her father is and how he treats her mother and herself. The point is that as long as girls must deal with inequality and with cultural sex-role stereotypes, fathers and daughters cannot easily relate to each other on the basis of their real personalities and needs.

The relationship of mother and daughter, to which we turn next, is similarly shaped by cultural constraints.

Notes

[1]This confusion may explain the recent publication of a number of books intended for the general reader that deal with fathering--*Father Power* by Henry Biller and Dennis Meredith (1974); *Who Will Raise the Children* by James Levine (1976); and with the male role in general--Marc Feigen-Fasteau's *The Male Machine;* (1974) and *Men and Masculinity,* by Joseph Pleck and Jack Sawyer (1974). In all these cases the authors are men who are concerned with undoing the constraints of traditional images of masculinity, particularly the obstacles to nurturance and expressiveness. Although the father-daughter relationship is not the major focus of these books, they contribute to creating a climate of opinion that may enable fathers to shape their relationships with their daughters according to mutual needs and interests rather than unnecessary or outmoded conventions and stereotypes.

[2]Clearly the widespread desire for male children affects reproductive patterns. Until a couple has a son, they may go on having children beyond the number ideally desired (Westoff, Potter, and Sagi, 1963). One study found that, when family size is taken into account, parents are more likely to have another child if they have all girls rather than all boys.

[3]A new movement within Judaism to find a ceremonial way of welcoming a girl child is described in a letter to the editors of *Ms.,* by Mickey Swerdlow, October, 1974.

[4]John Whiting points out that in polygamous societies where brides are costly, a man with only sons would become poverty-stricken; he needs to have daughters as well (personal communication, 1975),

[5]For men, physical expressions of affection are seen as connoting heterosexual interest if addressed to females and homosexual tendencies if expressed toward other men. These restrictions often generalize, making it difficult for many to feel comfortable expressing tender feelings. The following anecdote is an illustration. At a celebration honoring the 90th birthday of Harvard Law School Professor Austin Scott, Erwin Griswold, the former Solicitor-General of the United States, felt compelled to say as preamble, "Men have a good deal of trouble in our society, somehow or other, in expressing affection for other men," before he could come out with, "Scotty, we love you" (*Harvard Gazette,* October, 1974). One gets the feeling it would have been even harder to say these words had the object of the affection not been of such a venerable age: observers have commented that sex-role restrictions in many societies become weaker as people age.

IV. Mothers and Daughters

Mother, may I go out to swim?
Yes, my darling daughter.
Hang your clothes on a hickory limb
And don't go near the water.

The variety of life patterns opening up for women, along with debate over the rewards and costs of such patterns, have combined to create uncertainty in many mothers about how to bring up their daughters. Often they worry about what the consequences will be for their daughters if they refuse to live out their lives in traditional ways. Although most would probably agree that the pattern endorsed by so many young women today--that of career and family--is a desirable one, they themselves have rarely fully resolved the difficulties associated with such a pattern. Those mothers who have established their competence in areas associated with men may have seemed in their own eyes and in the eyes of others as in some way deviant or peculiar as women and incompetent as mothers; those who have lived in a traditional way may have found themselves and their lifestyles devalued. Yet the very turmoil of change can be an asset. Women who are themselves engaged in re-examining their own assumptions and choices can, whatever their ultimate decisions, use their experiences to help their daughters make choices considerably freer from social constraints than were their own.

In most families, patterns of mother-daughter relationships, set in motion at infancy and derived in part from the mother's own experiences in growing up, are important determinants of girls' competence. The mother is typically both the first socializer and teacher and the most available model of womanhood; she can hardly escape being a major influence on her daughter's behavior, attitudes, and aspirations. In this chapter, we analyze some of the social and psychological forces that complicate the mother's efforts toward developing competence in girls and suggest some approaches to overcoming them; and reflect on the implications for mother-daughter relationships of the traditional maternal role pattern. Variations in this pattern, especially that of the employed mother, are considered in Chapter 7. Let us begin by examining the role of mother in various places and various periods.

The Role of Mother: An Anthropological Overview

Those who study cross-cultural differences in the role of women, especially the role of mother, do not always agree about the relative quality of life for modern Western women. Some anthropologists, pointing to the greater participation of women in rituals and in social, artistic, and political life in many less developed societies, present and past, conclude that, by comparison, the life of the suburban housewife is isolated and impoverished (C.B. Lloyd, 1975; B.B. Whiting,

1977). In those rural societies where males often leave their farms and families to work in urban employment, for instance, women retain considerable control of the family's economic resources and thus enjoy power and prestige. And where children are both scarce and looked upon as assets, women have relatively high status as producers of valuable resources.

A contrasting view of women in less developed societies can be found in the proceedings of the 1975 International Women's Year Conference. Take the following account of a day in the life of one Zambian woman, which illustrates the lot of millions of the world's women:

> She wakes at 5 a.m., eats little or nothing, straps her baby on her back and walks a mile to a field. There, for 10 hours, she bends and stoops, planting or hoeing. At 3 p.m., she scavenges for firewood and carries it and her child back home. There she pounds grain kernels into meal and prepares other food. By 6 p.m. she is ready for another walk—this one a three mile round trip—to fetch water (*New York Times,* June 26, 1976).

Even projects designed to raise the living standard in the developing countries often have the opposite effect upon women. When chickens were introduced into one village, they too needed water:

> So, besides carrying water for their families, village women had to carry much more to water the chickens, increasing their daily workload (*Idem*).

All else being equal, the status of women and the valuation of motherhood are highest when the role of mother is linked to production and control of economic resources--children, food, money--and to decision-making processes (Rosaldo & Lamphere, 1974). For approximately ninety percent of our species' time on earth, human beings have lived in hunter-gatherer societies. In these societies, small groups of people roamed from place to place, depending upon the season of the year and the supply of food, setting up temporary homesites as they went. For most women, in such societies, the combination of a short life-span and high infant mortality meant that child-bearing and rearing were a central theme throughout their adult lives; yet much of the mother's time and energy was inevitably spent in productive activities essential for the continued survival of her family. Part-time "child-care" was provided by older siblings; children were a valued resource. Thus both men and women derived a sense of importance from their varying forms of economic productivity and from full participation in the group's social life (Whiting, 1977).

With the advent of herding and limited agriculture, families began to establish a permanent residence. In contrast to the nomadic habits of the hunters and gatherers, herders often left their families at the residence for extended periods of time. Women then took on such activities as growing crops within the immediate vicinity of the residence, and maintaining the residence itself. Although wives were no longer major providers, both parents had important and complementary roles in maintaining the viability of their families (C.B. Lloyd, 1975).

Such a life-style can be compared in some ways to that of early periods in American history. Until the 1800s, at least, women in pioneer communities worked along with men. Herding and agriculture were the primary occupations. With families often isolated from one another, each had of necessity to be relatively self-sufficient. Men worked the fields or tended the animals; pioneer mothers, though they made relatively little contribution to food production or acquisition, became increasingly responsible for food preparation and such subsistence activities as making clothing and other necessities. An entry from the diary of Abigail Foote in

Massachusetts in 1775 gives a glimpse of the variety of these tasks:

> Fix'd gown for Prude--Mend Mother's Riding-hood--Spun short thread--fix'd two gowns for Welsh's girls--Carded tow--Spun linen--Worked on Cheese basket, Hatchel'd flax with Hannah, we did 51 lbs. a piece--Milked the cows--Spun linen, did 50 knots--Made a broom of Guinea-wheat straw--Spun thread to whiten--Set a red dye--Had two scholars from Mrs. Taylor's--I carded two pounds of wool and felt Nationly--Spun harness twine, scoured the pewter (Cited in S. Lloyd, in press).

With the coming of industrialization and the gradual physical separation of home and work, important productive aspects of woman's role diminished. Mass-produced clothing, for example, became readily available. During the second half of the 19th century, this growing industrialization had major repercussions on family life and on the role of the mother. Families left the farm and moved to the city; men learned new skills and earned their livelihood at jobs distant from their homes; children left home at an early age to work or to be educated by strangers who could teach them the skills necessary to function in this new environment; with all of this, the mother's productive role decreased markedly. Perhaps the greatest change was that children, so highly valued in agricultural society, were now becoming a potential drain on family resources. With industrialization, children were indeed costly; the family had to pay for their food, clothing, and education. Decreases in infant mortality, furthermore, meant that one did not need to have so many children to assure the survival of a few and thus the continuity of the family. The economic interdependence between husband and wife was increasingly undermined. A man who was not a farmer and had only a few children was less dependent on his wife than she was on him.

Amidst all these changes the one pattern retained was that the mother stayed close to home. She was still responsible for caring for the children, preparing the family's food, and maintaining the household, but because of modern technology these required less time and fewer skills. In addition, the affluence resulting from the advent of modern technology, the concern about over-population, and the lengthening life span combined to undermine and devalue the role of mother even further. Functions that in earlier days and in other cultures had earned mothers status, satisfaction, and respect now earned them few such rewards. High status and respect, on the contrary, came to be associated with success outside the home in arenas to which women had no ready access. Women were neither prepared for nor encouraged to participated in prestigious work; they were instead socialized to believe that the very qualities associated with success in those activities were unfeminine. Traits such as competence, assertiveness, and business-like efficiency were for them, they were told, masculine and undesirable, evidence of inadequacy as a woman and of unfitness for motherhood.

The Recent Past

Because economic dependence is inherent in the role of mother as it has evolved historically, a woman in such a position often feels insecure and may attempt to make herself indispensable to her husband and children (Thompson, 1949). There is no end to the demands of young children nor to what one can do to enhance their lives; thus many such women can and do make motherhood a full-time job. One such mother, who participated in a study comparing professional women and homemakers (Birnbaum, 1975), gives us a revealing look at some of the consequences. Subjects were asked to make up a story starting with the cue, "Now that her youngest child is starting school, Lois..."

> Ten years of tending little children, always having someone needing your attention, ten years of being "mom" first and foremost. These days are over at last. Billy was starting kindergarten and Lois was free to be her own master for those school hours...Now that all four little ones were off and away, what was mother to do? The long desired moments to relax in the morning with the paper, not swiftly glancing at it before bed. Time now to be creative, contribute to the community, be an individual, but where to start, what to concentrate on? Lois felt free--but somehow at loose ends. Her husband, Peter, noticed the change...the change was a turmoil. Lois went from one thing to another never really accomplishing anything, rushing to be home when school was out--to be there--ready to chauffeur to lessons of all sorts and other extra-curricular activities (p. 408).

After World War II this child-centered view of the family, with particular focus on the role of the mother, reached a peak. Studies of children orphaned or separated from parents by the war underlined the critical role of mothering in normal psychological and physical development. Child-care professionals, horrified by the consequences of maternal deprivation, added unwittingly to the psychological burden of mothers. Those who observed institutionalized babies and young children--Anna Freud (Freud & Burlingham, 1944); John Bowlby (1969); and René Spitz (1945)--concluded that since children are damaged by separation from their mothers, they require, from birth, an uninterrupted relationship with one person--the mother. Although conceding that the severity and permanence of the damage to institutionalized children depended upon the age of the child, the duration of separation, and above all the qualities of substitute care, they clear-

ly implied that mothers who wanted to pursue interests outside of the home risked similar consequences for their
children. Out of concern for the child, a good mother should
willingly subordinate her needs to meet those of her child
(Spock, 1946). Loving one's child and loving to take exclusive
care of one's child became one and the same. Any mother
who had negative reactions to this pattern was vulnerable to
feelings of deviance, guilt and inadequacy. Yet mothers of
dependent children have been entering the labor force in increasing numbers since World War II (Nye, 1974), and this
despite such social supports as government welfare policies
designed to keep mothers at home. By 1975, approximately
one out of every two married women with children six
through seventeen years was working, as were more than one-
third of the women with preschool children. Indications are
that this trend will persist. The increasing numbers of women
receiving higher education, the rise in the median age at
which first marriages are taking place, and the steadily declining birth rate suggest that more and more women are determined to qualify themselves before marriage for some form
of paid employment thereafter.

That mothers are a major force in our labor market,
however, has as yet had impact neither on social definitions
of the role of mother nor on related social policies. Debates
over government support for child-care services, indeed,
reflect a family "domino" theory: financial aid to day-care
centers will entice women out of the home; the family will fall
apart; crime will increase; and so on. Previous shifts in social
and economic realities, however, have inevitably been
associated, as we have seen, with dramatic changes in the
value of the role of mother. Current changes in social attitudes toward women, and growing acceptance of women in
high-status positions, will equally surely cause a redefinition
of the maternal role. Traditional attitudes and patterns, and
thus ambiguity and confusion, will nevertheless be with us for

a long time. The consequences for daughters need to be understood.

The Traditional Mother-Daughter Relationship

> *I wish you first a baby boy*
> *and when his hair begins to curl*
> *I wish you next a baby girl.*

Women who were socialized to be traditional mothers, whether or not they live out that pattern, bring to their relationships with their daughters certain attitudes and practices which may affect their daughter's competence. To begin with, men and women even today prefer to have a male for their first child (Dinitz et al., 1954; Westoff & Rindfuss, 1974). When women prefer not to reproduce their own sex, one must ask why. The answer lies at least in part in the relatively inferior status of women in our culture, a status with many ramifications. Many women have low regard for other women; many express a preference to be male (Brown, 1957). Disappointment at the thought of producing another inferior being would naturally follow. Having a son to identify with is a way to compensate for inferiority and to satisfy vicariously needs whose fulfillment is blocked to women in our culture, as Adrienne Rich (1976) shows us in a passage from *Of Woman Born:*

When I first became pregnant I set my heart on a son. (In our childish 'acting-out' games I had always preferred the masculine roles and persuaded or forced my younger sister to act the feminine ones.) I still identified more with men than with women; the men I knew seemed less held back by self-doubt and ambivalence, more choices seemed open to them. I wanted to give birth, at twenty-five, to my unborn self... someone independent, actively willing, original (p. 193).

One wonders about the consequences for daughters of such deep-seated feelings. Here is another example poignantly expressed in a note to Ann Landers:

> A few months ago I gave birth to my second daughter. I am convinced that I will never have a son and I would rather die, I mean it literally, than face another pregnancy...I just want to raise our two girls.

> Why does society make the mother who has produced only girls feel that she has failed her husband and is missing out on life's greatest joy...I also know that the sex of a child is determined by the male and not the female.

> None of this helps (*Boston Globe,* December 11, 1974).

An extreme example of the consequences of being a girl in a culture that values boys comes in a report from the United Nations Food and Agriculture Organization:

> More than half [of the world's women] live in rural villages in poor countries. To be born female there is, in most cases, to be born an underdog...The birth of a female is often viewed as a disaster, but the birth of a male child is cause for joy in all cultures... Boys are seen by parents as the chief hope for security in old age. Girls, on the other hand, will become attached to some other family. Consequently, boys are favored with care and food. Infant mortality for girls is much higher. Just getting enough food to allow young bodies and minds to fully develop--so that they are capable of learning and working--is a struggle in most poor villages. If there are shortages, females are the most likely to eat less...If health care is available and if a family can afford it, males generally receive it first. When it is time for school--if education is available at

all--boys are again favored. (*New York Times*, June 26, 1975).

   Regardless of preference, just over 50% of babies are born female. Once presented with this reality, fortunately, even women with strong wishes for a son are usually able to develop warm relationships with their daughters. Indeed, it appears that daughters provide somewhat greater and more socially acceptable opportunities than do sons for mothers to express their nurturant, protective feelings. Despite the inconclusive nature of scientific evidence concerning differential treatment of sons and daughters,[1] most observers agree that social expectations, innate qualities of female infants, and maternal attitudes interact to influence the mother-daughter relationship in ways significantly different from the mother-son relationship. Female babies at birth, we know, are seen as more delicate than male infants although the females are actually sturdier and more mature physically (Rubin *et al.*, 1974). This misperception, which fits popular images of female fragility, may make mothers anxious about their daughters' well-being and endurance. Mothers in fact do tend to handle male babies more vigorously than females, with whom they interact in more verbal modes (Moss, 1967).
   Female babies may differ from their male counterparts in ways that affect the mother-daughter relationship. Infant girls, we learn from several studies, respond more readily to sights and sounds, have a relatively high threshold for pain, and are more easily comforted (Garai & Scheinfeld, 1968). All this suggests that a baby girl is likely to react positively to her mother's presence. For most mothers, especially those anxious about their ability to care properly for a baby, such a response can be very reassuring; it rewards the mother in a meaningful way for attending to her daughter's needs. If the mother responds rapidly and regularly to her daughter's cries, the baby soon learns that her mother is her source of

comfort. Both mother and daughter may thus create a mutually dependent relationship. In fact, mothers of girls are more likely than mothers of boys to give attention in response to their child's crying without waiting to respond at a time of her own choosing (Moss, 1967).

This interdependence between mothers and daughters, learned so early, continues. By the age of two, according to Michael Lewis and his colleagues, girls show different patterns of behavior towards their mothers and their fathers. With their mothers, girls are more demonstratively affectionate--hugging, touching, and kissing them; with their fathers they are more distant--smiling, talking, and looking at them. Mothers engage in and thus encourage more physical closeness with their daughters than with their sons (Lewis, Weinraub, & Ban, 1972). Such a continuing reinforcement of dependent behavior may reflect a feeling that it is unnecessary to encourage independent behavior in little girls. The pattern is particularly likely to occur among women whose own dependence has never been discouraged.

Mothers of four-year-old girls, additional data suggest, set later target dates for granting autonomy to their daughters than do mothers of boys of that age. When asked at what age they believed parents should allow a child to use sharp scissors with no adult supervision, mothers of daughters gave significantly later ages than did mothers of sons (Collard, 1964). These findings are consistent with the themes of caution and overprotection in mothers' behavior toward daughters (Hoffman, 1972).

Data we have recently collected from white, middle-class mothers of four-year old girls and boys suggest that maternal attitudes toward independence granting may be changing (Barnett & Baruch, 1977). There were essentially no differences between mothers of daughters and mothers of sons in the age at which they expected their children to be able to do such things as riding a two-wheel bicycle to a friend's house across a fairly busy street, or going to the movies unaccompanied by an adult. In more subtle ways, however, today's mothers may still expect their sons to be more sturdy and more capable of independent behavior and may behave toward them in such a way as to make these expectations come true. Such encouragement and reinforcement are undoubtedly picked up by the young boy and reflected in his growing picture of himself as a confident and competent individual. Quite different are the mothers' expectations for and reactions to their daughters, as well as the girls' feelings about their own abilities. What results is often a self-fulfilling prophecy of dependency, intensified by the tendency of many fathers to reward dependent behavior in their daughters (Osofsky & O'Connell, 1972).

In sum, a large body of evidence suggests that during the first three or four years of life, girls and boys receive different training with respect to dependency and autonomy. What are the effects, if any, of these differences? According to the psychologist Lois Hoffman (1972), girls, during the nursery school years, are more conforming, suggestible, dependent on the opinions of others than boys, more likely to withdraw from frustrating situations, more anxious to please adults, and more willing to work for adult approval. Such approval-seeking and dependence limit both the kinds of experiences girls seek and those that adults provide for them. Early patterns of interaction between mother and daughter, then, perhaps because they are consistent with images of femininity, may be maintained well beyond the age during which dependency serves a useful purpose. One longitudinal study found that, for women but not for men, childhood dependence was a good predictor of adult dependence; in women dependency, a sex-appropriate trait, remained relatively stable (Kagan and Moss, 1962).

Mother as Role Model

For a girl in a traditional family, the role of mother is the central one toward which she is taught to aspire. The role model most readily available to a young girl to facilitate this process of anticipatory socialization is of course her mother. One way by which children prepare themselves for those adult roles that they hope to attain is, according to sociologist Robert Merton, by imitating the behaviors and attitudes of people currently in those roles (Merton & Kitt, 1950). By such "rehearsal" young people prepare themselves to move smoothly into new roles.

Some mothers, however, are currently questioning whether they want their daughters to follow the life paths that they themselves have chosen. Some have expressed the wish that their daughters marry later than they did and that they evaluate the pros and cons of having children rather than having them just because of society's expectations (Barnett & Baruch, 1978). Whether and how these hopes will affect the process of anticipatory socialization remains to be seen.

The mother also plays her part in the child's growing understanding of such concepts as "female" and "mother." There is considerable evidence that once children understand which sex they belong to, they want to see themselves as being like others of the same sex (Kohlberg, 1966). For developing the cognitive as well as emotional elements of a sense of identity, this desire is crucial. A problem for many girls is the fact that this drive often conflicts with an equally strong drive to identify with that parent who is powerful, has high status, and controls the family's resources--most often the father (Bronfenbrenner, 1960; Kagan, 1958; J.W. Whiting, 1960).Preschoolers, we learn from research, see their mothers as almost exclusively involved in activities within the home--cleaning, washing, ironing, cooking, and caring for the children. Compared to their fathers, who are seen as more dominant, smarter, and as "the boss," mothers seem less competent and strong (Hartley & Klein, 1959; Kagan & Lemkin, 1960). Very young children's cognitive limitations may also lead them to assume that fathers are smarter because they are bigger, have larger heads, and therefore have bigger brains (Kohlberg & Ullian, 1974).

There is some evidence, on the other hand, that girls reared in households in which the mother has important decision-making and economic responsibilities are more likely to see the mother as a strong and competent figure. This we shall deal with in Chapter 7.

The Adolescent Crisis

Much of the above discussion has focused on the early years of a girl's life, but another crucial period for the growth of competence in girls is adolescence. During these years, an inclination to win peer approval by acting in accordance with social conventions may well conflict with the development of a clear sense of one's own identity and individuality.

Adolescence is an especially difficult time for many girls. Successes in school which have won them recognition by teachers and parents may now seem to teenaged girls inappropriate and unfeminine; peer approval, so highly valued, is rarely given to such pursuits. By the high-school years, then, many girls are anxious about whether academic success will bring social isolation and loss of femininity--concerns too often echoed rather than alleviated by their mothers. The women executives studied by Margaret Hennig (1970) reported that at puberty, just when they were beginning to suffer from the restrictions placed on them as girls, their mothers began to exert pressure on them to be "feminine":

When I was about twelve, I decided that my mother

wasn't really all I had her stacked up to be. I remember
it was a terrible crisis in my life. I think it all began after
she began to suggest that I give up my tomboy status.
She said I should settle down and learn to become a
young lady - that word "learn" struck home with me! I
thought it was very nice to be a young lady but not the
way my mother meant it. She meant being a "young
lady;" I looked upon myself as a person (p. 47).

Because of her own uncertain direction, a mother may be
unable to facilitate her daughter's growth at this time. If she
has been dissatisfied with her own life, a traditional mother
may want to encourage her daughter to prepare for a career;
yet she may hesitate to do so for fear of exposing her
daughter to criticism, frustration, or failure. Then too, a
mother who is overly tied to her daughter and to her own
need to be needed may have difficulties with, or may not be
able to acknowledge, her daughter's initial attempts at a
separate identity and may fail to support her efforts toward
autonomy. Other women may view their daughters'
movements toward a different life style as rejection of them,
and so react with hostility.

A mother's reaction to her adolescent daughter may also be
colored by her response to her daughter's emerging sexuality.
Psychoanalysts have made much of the renewed sexual interests among adolescents in their opposite-sex parents.
Whether or not this is a factor in a particular family, the
potential for rivalry between a mother and daughter is certainly present, perhaps especially in cultures like ours where
women are prized for a youthful appearance. Under these circumstances, a middle-aged woman may compare herself
negatively to her teen-aged daughter. In the absence of other
sources of self-esteem, advancing age can heighten a
woman's sense of vulnerability and insecurity, leading her to
withdraw emotional support from her closest competitor, her
daughter.

Mothers of Competent Daughters

Unfortunately, researchers at present have little concrete advice to offer mothers who wish to avoid the patterns described above. There are, however, a few relevant studies. Diana Baumrind and her colleagues (Baumrind, 1971; Baumrind & Black, 1967) are following into later years a group of girls (and boys) first studied as pre-schoolers. Mothers of the competent pre-school girls typically showed both warmth and firmness toward their daughters, directly expressing displeasure at misbehavior, consistently enforcing rules, setting high standards for mature behavior. They were neither overly permissive nor rigidly authoritarian; they neither gave in to their daughter's demands nor suppressed open discussion of differences. Thus the girls were able to express resistance or anger, but were held to firm standards.

This maternal pattern is remarkably similar to the description given by Stanley Coopersmith (1968) of parents of children (in this case pre-adolescent boys) with high self-esteem. Such parents, he found, were accepting of their children and respected their individuality, but they also set and enforced clear demands and limits. Demands and limits provide valuable feedback about the environment, enabling the child to behave in ways that are rewarding and thus enhance self-esteem. Parents of high self-esteem boys, moreover, particularly valued independence and assertiveness in their children, in contrast to parents of low self-esteem boys who valued such traits as kindness and compliance--qualities by which girls have typically been socialized. It appears that bringing up girls to be considerate and conforming, rather than assertive and independent, may not be conducive to self-esteem. Indeed, in a study of pre- and postadolescent girls, Baruch (1976) found that girls who perceived themselves as competent were more likely to have mothers who valued such traits as independence and assertiveness (both in their daughters and in themselves) than were the girls who did not see themselves as competent.

Mothers who have exemplified these traits in their own lives often have profoundly positive effects upon their daughters' lives. In Margaret Mead's account of her early career she recalls:

> My earliest field trip was with my mother when she was doing graduate research on Italian-Americans...Years later I did my master's thesis in psychology at Columbia on the children of the families she studied (Harris, 1970).

A warning is necessary at this point. There is a difference between openness to change and adaptiveness to new opportunities on the one hand and rigorous prescription of new conventions on the other. It would be damaging to mothers and daughters alike if a different set of stereotypes, social demands, and anxieties increasingly gave rise to the dilemma described by one daughter of a professional mother.

> As I grew older and people commented on how much my mother had achieved, raising four children, teaching, doing research, and all that, it seemed strange to me that they would think this unusual. That was my idea of what a mother did...I think it has set a hard pattern for me. I do not have any strong career drives. I want to marry and have children. But I fear that won't be enough for me. I'll feel that I have to have some kind of career, for you can't just shake off a pattern like that even if you want to (Bernard, 1966, p. 224).

The best thing a mother can do for herself and her daughter is to assign the highest priority to enriching her own life and increasing the satisfactions she derives from it, while remaining open-minded about the way her daughter chooses to fulfill the needs and capacities of her own separate personality.

Notes

[1]The debate about this evidence can be followed by reading Maccoby and Jacklin (1974), Block (1975), and Hoffman (1977).

V. Marital and Family Patterns: Themes and Variations

Magazines, newspapers, and television currently provide us with an overwhelming array of new "lifestyles" to consider: unmarried couples who live together, divorced fathers with custody of their children, single women who adopt children-- all treated as fascinating experiments proliferating at a time when old patterns are breaking up and when people increasingly believe in the possibility of choosing among new ones.

Evidence of shifts in patterns is strong indeed. In 1976 husband-wife households constituted only about 67% of all families, compared with 71% in 1969. One in three adults was either divorced, widowed, or never married; and 13% of all households were headed by females. The number of adults under 35 who live alone has more than doubled since 1970, a trend attributed to: a tendency among young persons to leave home earlier and marry later; a rising divorce rate; and "the growing career ambitions of women" (*New York Sunday Times,* March, 20, 1977).

According to a Labor Department survey, "The old-fashioned 'typical American family' with a breadwinner husband, a homemaker wife, and two children, now makes up only 7% of the nation's families (*Boston Globe,* March 8, 1977):'' Thus changes in labor-force participation are occurring along with changes in marital and family patterns. In 1975, 44% of all married women were working, as were 37% of women with children under 6; in 1960, the comparable figures were 31% and 19% respectively. The chances are increasingly slim that a woman will live in accordance with the cultural norm; marry young; have at least two children relatively quickly; stay at home to raise them until they leave; live happily ever after with her original husband.

The entry of women into the paid work force is a phenomenon that both reflects and generates social changes. The participation of women in the labor force is associated with their increased educational attainment, with rising divorce rates, and with falling birth rates. Women are marrying later in life than previously, and a growing number remain single and/or childless (Glick, 1975).

In this chapter we shall address two related topics: the impact of changing marital and family patterns on the development of women's competence; and vice versa, the impact of growing competence on family patterns.

Theories of Marriage and the Family

Though it is customary to discuss marriage and the family together, the two social institutions are in fact distinct, each having a long and fascinating history, each having an impact on the other. Contrary to the popular idea that the forms we know today are eternal, they are in fact relatively recent (Ariès, 1962). Marriage, the formal, legal union of man and woman, is one of the world's oldest and most enduring institutions; yet the great variety of marital patterns currently found across the world attests to the flexibility inherent in the concept. Our culture differs from many in that marriage in its ideal form implies not only a long-term commitment but sexual exclusivity. Families, too, have a variety of forms. In our own culture, there are families that are large and small, close-knit and estranged, single-parent and two-parent. In other cultures families may be, for example, matrilocal or patrilocal, nuclear or extended. And marital and family patterns differ in their impact upon women's competence.

Before analyzing these differences we need to place them in the context of theories about the nature of males and females and about the proper relationship between them.

Theoretical Perspectives on Marital and Family Patterns

The Genetic View. One of the major dimensions along which theories of marriage and the family vary is the degree to which innate sex differences are seen as legitimate determinants of social roles. The famous psychologist E.L. Thorndike (1903) endorsed the genetic viewpoint:

> The most striking difference in instinctive equipment consists in the strength of the fighting instinct in the male and of the nursing instinct in the female. No one will doubt that men are more possessed by the instinct to fight, to be the winner in games and serious contests, than are women; nor that women are more possessed than men by the instinct to nurse, care for... The existence of these two instincts has long been recognized by literature and common knowledge, but their importance in causing differences in the general activities of the sexes has not. The fighting instinct is in fact the cause of a very large amount of the world's intellectual endeavors (p. 118-119).

The genetic argument, one can see, is not just that women are innately very different from men but that men's biological endowments make them suited for certain positions, those associated with power, leadership, and dominance. It follows that men are unsuited for those roles for which a woman's biological endowment prepares her, particularly child-rearing. Women who aspire to positions of power and men who wish to play a major role in the care of their children are therefore behaving "unnaturally. "

Despite impressive contradictory evidence, this point of view has had a profound and continuing effect on Western thought. Such tenacity raises serious questions as to the purely "scientific" nature of a theoretical perspective long used to justify what has been called the essence of inequality, "the social division of labor based on gender"(Dixon, 1976). Those opposed to the genetic viewpoint are forced to address again the old question of the adequacy of women for positions of competence and power, particularly the issue of women's mental capacity. Note the following passage by the sociologist Cynthia Epstein:

> The existence of a large stratum of educated, trained, and professionally active women make it unnecessary to argue the question of women's innate intellectual capacity or their ability to sustain high-concentration work. The question of whether women are as intelligent as men, or whether or not they can handle abstract ideas and solve abstract problems, has been eliminated by their achievements in mathematics, chemistry, physics, and the social sciences. Although the extent of women's capacities is still argued at dinner tables, in newspaper columns, and by educators, the truth is that women *do*, therefore women *can* (1971b, 121-125).

Parsons' Sociological Theory. Talcott Parsons' analysis of marriage (1955) has been perhaps the most influential among behavioral scientists. In his view, the roles of husband and wife encompass mutually exclusive functions. The husband's role comprises those activities that tie the couple or family to the larger social system; they are "instrumental," and include earning a living, conducting transactions, representing the family in the community. The role of the wife centers around such "expressive" functions as maintaining a favorable emotional climate for the family, nurturing and caring for her children, and providing emotional support for her husband. Parsons' description is also prescriptive; he believes that the solidarity and well-being of the conjugal family is facilitated by a rigid sex-linked division of labor:

> By confining the number of status-giving occupational roles of the members of the effective conjugal unit to one, it eliminates any competition for status, especially as between husband and wife which might be disruptive of the solidarity of marriage. So long as lines of achievement are segregated and not directly comparable, there is less opportunity for jealousy, a sense of inferiority, etc., to develop.

Such a narrow conception of the roles of husbands and wives ignores such "wifely" activities as those of consumer, bill payer, committee member, volunteer worker, organizer, along with the role of husband in such "expressive" functions as child-care and other nurturant activities.

Parsons' ideas stem from an era when "traditional" ideals of marriage were rarely challenged. Evidence is now accumulating that deviations from this model do not necessarily cause the marital tensions and dissolutions that Parsons feared. Let us turn to this issue.

The Radical Feminist View. The thinking of radical feminists begins with two basic postulates: the economic oppression of women; and the conflict, past and present, between men and women. Their analysis of marriage grows out of Engel's insights into the economic basis of the course of history; however, they argue that sexual distinctions rather than economic events underlie all historic events. Rephrasing Engels, the radical feminist Shulamith Firestone writes:

> Historical materialism is that view of the course of history which seeks the ultimate cause and the great moving power of all historic events in the dialectic of sex: the division of society into two distinct biological classes for procreative reproduction and the struggles of these classes with one another; in the changes in the modes of marriage, reproduction and childcare; on the related development of other physically-differentiated classes (castes); and in the first division of labor based on sex which developed into the (economic, cultural) class system (1971, p. 12).

With respect to marriage, the radical feminists' position, as given by Sheila Cronan, is:

> Since marriage constitutes slavery for women, it is clear that the Women's Movement must concentrate on attacking this institution. Freedom for women cannot be won without the abolition of marriage (1973, p. 219).

The biological family--especially in its present form, the nuclear family--functions as the perpetrator of sexual inequality. Technological advances that lessen the viability and necessity of perpetuating the biological family thus win praise from such writers as these.

The three points of view just discussed draw attention to certain nearly universal features of marriage: a sex-linked division of labor and the association of power, status, and decision-making with the male role.[1] Although the specific tasks assigned to the sexes vary widely from culture to culture--except for those associated with the role of warrior or hunter--the tasks most highly valued in any culture are those that males perform. For this reason, both researchers and activists have become aware that eliminating inequality requires not only the entry of women into the public sphere but deepening involvement by men in domestic life, particularly child care.

According to the economist Cynthia Lloyd (1975) "Marriage as an institution has evolved from and been reinforced by the original economic advantage of a sexual division of labor." But in our society this economic advantage, and indeed the "economic underpinnings of marriage, have been eroded." Thus greater variation in the division of labor can be expected; and because this division creates, as well as reflects, differences in skills, changes will affect women's and men's competence in the various spheres of life. The man who cares for his child becomes more skillful as a parent; the woman who is a wage earner becomes more sophisticated about economic issues. Particularly in middle-class families such change is already under way.

The Changing American Middle-Class Family

Despite social-class differences in the structure of marital and family roles,[2] most Americans have shared a common image of what is desirable in family life, one that has important implications for women's competence. The image depicts a husband devoted to the advancements of his own career, working in an organization located away from his household; a wife who is not employed, although her educational level is usually similar to that of her husband; and more than one child. The wife's need for achievement is met partly through taking credit for the accomplishments of her children and partly through the phenomenon labeled by Jean Lipman-Blumen (1972) as "vicarious achievement:" the wife identifies with her husband's career accomplishments as if they were her own. Indeed, her identification is sometimes translated into actual participation in his work in a supportive and unpaid capacity, thus creating the "two-person career" (Papaneck, 1973).

This pattern is found at all occupational levels. The wife of the Fuller Brush man writes his orders; the ambassador's wife entertains visiting dignitaries. In her autobiography, Halina Rodzinski (1976) reports that shortly after her husband, Artur Rodzinski, was appointed conductor of the Cleveland Orchestra, she faced an important test of "whether I would be the proper social complement to his glamorous life and thus consolidate his position" (p. 111). Her successful first meeting with the orchestra's socially prominent trustees delighted her husband: "Halina, I'm so happy. You have won everyone's heart. Now I can concentrate on my work, while you take care of all the social nonsense that goes with the job" (p. 113). She also had backstage duties at his concerts. During intermission, she was expected to "give him an alcohol rub and... dry his thick hair with a brush and hot air dryer" (p. 108).

The lives of children as well as of wives are powerfully affected by demands of the husband's career. Organizations transfer male employees and their families on short notice, for instance, to locations chosen by the organizations, usually without regard to family preference. Children are expected to adjust to these changes in residence, and it is the wife's job to cope with any difficulties.

Clearly women's increasing participation in the labor force creates pressures for changes in the model just described, both in the norms and in the actual behavior associated with such a model. A career-oriented wife is often unable and unwilling to follow the stereotype; her decision to exercise competence in the occupational sphere thus affects marital and family patterns. The second part of this chapter deals with these effects.

The Impact on Marital Patterns

According to Parsons' theory, a wife's entry into the occupational world, because it breaks down role specialization, would inevitably create competitiveness and divisiveness within the family. Clearly her entry is not without profound effects. Researchers find less role specialization and more sharing of power in families where wives are wage earners, especially if their occupations are prestigious (Hoffman, 1960; Wallston, 1973). The wife's influence in decision-making increases in relation to the number of years she has worked since her marriage (Blood & Wolfe, 1960).

Do these differences affect marital happiness and satisfaction? Researchers disagree. The consequences when husband and wife share the roles of economic provider and of caretaker of children and home are still in dispute. David Lynn (1974) reports that men who participate in such arrangements are less happy with their marriages than are men who do not. The sociologist Alice Rossi, however, argues that:

> If anything greater similarity in family and occupation roles would add zest and vitality to the relations between men and women and minimize the social segregation of the sexes (1971, p. 120).

According to a recent large-scale survey of married women who were college graduates, employed wives were more satisfied with their marriages than were unemployed wives; husbands of both groups were equally satisfied (Campbell, Converse, & Rogers, 1976). Nevertheless, women's changing roles have raised many concerns. Most recently, male impotence has been the worry--a likely reaction, we are told, of men to independent and assertive, particularly sexually assertive, wives (Smith, 1971, cited in Lynn, 1974). Lynn's own assessment of the impact of the women's movement is pessimistic:

> [Their] causes are on the whole just, but that, in the short run, casualties in the form of human misery from the conflict brought about by the movement will be high indeed...Many women are living with latent frustration and anger that will be released when they become fully aware of their inferior position...One could argue that underlying rage is as bad as open rage. This may be true for the mental health of the angry woman, but it is probably not true for the stability of man-woman relationships (1974, p. 135).

Several researchers interested in the question of husband-wife relationships have carried out intensive studies of what is becoming labeled as "the dual-career couple," where both partners are highly committed to careers.[3] Lynda Holstrom (1972), studying a small sample of such couples in the United States, noted a weakening of old assumptions about the priority of the husband's career. Decisions about geographical locations, for one thing, took into account the needs of both partners.[4] The women studied by Holstrom noticed their own lack of envy of their husband's opportunities and achievements. Indeed, in another study, that of Birnbaum (1975), the highest marital satisfaction was found among professional women who worked full time and were highly committed to their careers. "Thus a favorite myth of family sociology is destroyed," comments the sociologist Constantina Safilios-Rothschild (1970), "namely, that married women work to compensate for an unhappy marriage."

Even though the wife's income increases a couple's affluence and relieves the husband of the heavy burden of being the sole economic provider, some men do resent the loss of power inherent in egalitarian marriages (Bernard, 1972; Holstrom, 1972). Clearly a husband's willingness to relinquish power and to take pride in his wife's successes are the prerequisites of a happy dual-career marriage.[5] Such husbands, according to Lotte Bailyn (1970), are likely to be family-oriented rather than dedicated solely to their work.

Even under favorable circumstances, couples who are devoted both to career and family must cope with many strains. Rona and Robert Rapoport (1971) studied dual-career couples in England and reported, for example, that a hectic daily pace, accompanied by a sense of "overload," is a frequent source of stress; in such households leisure is an extremely rare commodity. Indeed, career women who are wives and mothers joke about their own need for a wife, someone to assist with errands, entertaining, and the myriad duties the traditional wife performs. But on balance, the Rapoports conclude, the new pattern:

> provides major sources of satisfaction while at the same time creating burdens. Each couple operates at a high level of strain but they have all chosen this as their style of life; and when contemplating other patterns they usually reject them as less satisfactory for themselves as individuals...(p. 278).

The dilemmas of dealing simultaneously with work, husband, and children can of course be overwhelming, leading a woman to avoid or to give up one or more of the three commitments. For women who do not wish to forfeit a career, the way to avoid the overload may be to remain single or divorce, remain childless or have only one child.

Remaining Unmarried. The spectre of the old maid still haunts many young women as they contemplate dedication to a career. In our society, the woman who does not marry is stigmatized as either too undesirable to have had the opportunity for marriage or as too peculiar to appreciate the superiority of the married state. In her book *Single Blessedness,* Margaret Adams (1976) points out that single women must constantly battle a sense of social insecurity. Yet for most of those she interviewed the desire for personal independence and autonomy was a chief motive for remaining single; most had had several opportunities to marry.

Indeed, it is the most competent women, according to Jessie Bernard (1972), who are likely to be selected *out of* marriage. The more income a woman earns, the less likely she is to marry. Bernard speculates that "a good job that pays well is a strong competitor to marriage for many women …And the girl who has the well-paying job may be too achievement-motivated to attract men" (p. 129). Although men and women both choose partners from the same social class and cultural background, she comments, "men tend to marry women slightly below them in such measurable items as age, education, and occupation, and presumably, in other as yet unmeasurable items as well." Given this "marriage gradient," there is no one for the men at the bottom to marry, no one who will look up to them; conversely, there is no one at the top for successful women to look up to, no men who are superior to them. "The result is that the never-married men tend to be 'bottom of the barrel' and the women 'cream of the crop.'" Creating more "cream" probably increases the numbers of never-married women.

What can such women expect in the way of "quality of life"? Assuming a lessening of the stigma of "spinsterhood," we can hope, according to the evidence, that the quality will be high, at least for women engaged in meaningful work. Margaret Adams found in her interviews with single women that work was their most important source of "personal integrity and identity." Among women in high-level jobs, as we have learned from the Birnbaum (1975) study, being single is associated with high levels of satisfaction and self-esteem. In their follow-up study of a sample of gifted women now in their 60's Sears and Barbee (1977) similarly found a high level of satisfaction among unmarried women, particularly those who had been in paid employment for a significant portion of their lives. For such women, marriage is not a prerequisite for well-being. Many are taking advantage too of new laws allowing single persons to adopt children, thus mitigating one of the major deprivations of the unmarried state. (Women with low levels of education or those who lack socially valued, occupationally useful skills, may, of course, experience being single much less positively.)

Single women with high-powered careers, must, of course, do without the asset of wifely assistance available to most of their male colleagues. In a recent article on state legislators *New York Times,* December 29, 1976), one otherwise happy woman listed the disadvantages of her single status. She had no family to send campaigning; no one to share the burdens of her work; daily chores were a problem:

> Even single men have secretaries and mothers...They find a woman somewhere to clean up after them. I don't feel I can ask any woman to do that...

Another state senator decided what she would do if asked for a family photograph for her campaign brochure: "Stand myself next to my exercise bicycle." Yet both saw being single as permitting them to concentrate on increasingly higher office without worrying about the effects on a family. And the expressed intent of increasing numbers of divorced women not to remarry suggests that the unmarried state carries with it benefits of freedom and flexibility.

Divorce. The simultaneous increase in the proportion of women entering the labor market and the proportion of women divorcing has lead many researchers to predicate a cause-and-effect link between these two phenomena. Women whose educational and occupational attainments are high are possibly less motivated to remain in an unsatisfying marriage than are women without adequate resources for independent living. Evidence about the quality of life for divorced women is conflicting, however. Some divorced women, but not all, share the views of one professor who said, "Frankly, being divorced has been a true asset in my career, something that would probably not be the case for a man" (Kotin, 1976). In an article entitled, "Divorce: Chance of a New Lifetime," Carol Brown and her colleagues (Brown, Feldberg, Fox, & Kohen, 1976) discussed both positive and negative aspects of divorce. Interviews with 30 women, all mothers of young children and all divorced at least a year, brought from the majority the report of a heightened sense of well-being derived from freedom from domestic routines and an "increased personal autonomy and sense of competence."[7] Most of the divorced women, however, suffered from the strain of rearing children alone: "I can't take a breather." Financial problems also were usually severe.

E. Mavis Hetherington (1976), who has been studying the "aftermath" of divorce, focusing on how young children and their parents adapt, is concerned that "the myth of romantic love is being replaced by the myth of romantic divorce." She found parents and children alike suffering from the aftermath; suffering typically was at a peak about one year after the divorce. The newly divorced woman faces many difficult tasks, from such concrete ones as the need to earn a living to the more complex issues of how to establish a social life. The most important influence on the well-being of divorced persons, Hetherington found, was the presence or absence of a satisfying heterosexual relationship.

Problems associated with child-rearing affected mothers and fathers equally but differently. While the pain of their status as an outsider often caused fathers to withdraw from contact with their children, mothers tended to have difficulty maintaining control over them. Many mothers were both overly commanding and remiss in following through on their orders. Because newly divorced mothers suffer from feeling incompetent in the maternal role, Hetherington has proposed (*New York Times,* December 31, 1976) concrete help with child-rearing problems might best serve their needs.

The Impact on Family Patterns

By remaining childless or by having a small family, the woman who chooses to devote herself to a career can reduce the "overload" discussed above. There is evidence that women are choosing these options; according to the demographer Paul Glick (1975), the projected fertility rate of women as of 1973 was 1.9 children per woman, compared with 3.8 in 1957.

Although increasing numbers of couples are remaining childless--about 10% at present--there is still a stigma attached to the married couple without children.[8] Yet research comparing the well-being of couples with and without children finds childless couples are no less happy or satisfied with their lives than are those who become parents (Campbell *et al.,* 1976).

Couples who choose to have only one child are subjected to perhaps even greater criticism than are the childless (Beckman, 1976). Since popular judgments regard them as acting against the best interests of their only child, they stand out as particularly selfish. Perhaps reflecting the increasing trend toward one-child families--from 6% in 1955 to 11% in 1975--a lively symposium on stereotypes and realities concerning the only child was held at the 1976 annual meeting of the American Psychological Association. Not least among the interesting facts to emerge was the high proportion of only children and of parents of only children among both participants and audience!

The negative stereotypes of only children are well-known--they are spoiled, selfish, lonely; the parents, the persons responsible for the only-child status, are assumed to be neurotic as well as selfish. For this bleak picture researchers found little support. Mothers of only children show no difference in personality traits from their counterparts with large families; they do tend to be more highly educated, to have a higher occupational level, and to have been older when their first child was born (Beckman, 1976; Falbo, 1976). In a study of a representative sample of 583 women aged 18-49, those with only children had as positive feelings toward their child as did parents of two or more children.[9] Only children themselves, the researchers found, also failed to live up to their negative stereotypes (Falbo, 1976); they are about as cooperative and competitive as children in any other family composition. One surprising finding, however, concerned their cognitive development. Their IQ scores tend to be higher than second- and later-borns but lower than first-borns, perhaps because they do not have the intellectual experience of serving as teacher to younger siblings (Claudy, 1976). Overall, however, there appears to be little reason for women who prefer to have one child to fear any negative effects from their choice.

The Question of Maternal Employment

The concern of many women (and men) about the impact of maternal employment on the quality of the mothering their children receive is reflected in numerous articles and books. We have already noted the fallacy of generalizing from the effects of prolonged parental deprivation to the part-day occupational absence of mothers and fathers (see Chapter 4). The question usually asked about mothers who are career women, according to Lois Hoffman (1974a), is "What kind

of mother is she, and how have her children turned out?''
The overall impression derived from research is generally
positive; studies comparing working and non-working
mothers tend to find particularly favorable effects for girls
whose mothers work (Baruch, 1972; Hoffman, 1960, 1974b;
Nye & Hoffman, 1963; Vogel, Broverman, Broverman,
Clarkson, & Rosenkrantz, 1970; Wallston, 1973). Daughters
whose mothers work, we are told,

> choose their mothers as models and as the person they
> most admire. Adolescent daughters of working
> mothers, particularly in the middle- and upper-
> socioeconomic groups, have been found to be active,
> autonomous girls who admire their mothers but are not
> unusually close-tied to them. For girls of all ages having
> a working mother contributes to a concept of the female
> role that includes less restriction and a wider range of
> activities, and a self-concept that incorporates these
> aspects of the female role. They usually approve of
> maternal employment, plan to work when they grow up
> and become mothers, and if they are old enough, they
> are more often employed themselves (Hoffman, 1974a).

Tied to the question of maternal employment is of course
the question of paternal involvement in child-rearing.
Though dividing child care equally between parents is an
ideal for many people, it is one that can seldom be realized.
Careers that demand long hours of commitment are likely to
interfere with such arrangements; indeed, working-class
couples who may sign up for different factory shifts are often
better able to share child care than are professional couples
(Lein, 1977). For such reasons, fathers only rarely prove to be
a significant child-care resource (Weingarten, 1974).

Day-care centers and after-school programs thus are the
most promising resources for the care of children. Initially
viewed as dangerous to family life and to children's optimal
development, they are now gaining acceptance. Studies of

centers providing high-quality care find no differences between young children who do and who do not spend partial
days at the centers with respect to intellectual development,
parent-child relationships (especially mother-child attachment) and social relationships with adults and peers
(Kagan, Kearsley, & Zelazo, 1976).[10] In the next chapter, we
turn to an examination of the impact of later schooling on the
development of competence in girls.

Notes

[1]For a provocative discussion of possible explanations for this pattern, see
Lipman-Blumen (1976).

[2]For analyses of social-class differences, see Komarovsky (1962) and Veroff
& Feld (1970).

[3]Those couples who have allowed themselves to be studied and who thus
can be described in this section, are, of course, a self-selected group and
therefore may not be typical. They are certainly not equivalent to the
"dual-work" couples whose jobs do not require the same level of ability
and commitment. Among other things, they are all intact families. Thus
those who divorced or separated, perhaps because they were unable to ac-
commodate to the strains imposed by this new kind of relationship, are not
included.

[4]The phenomenon of "commuting couples" is beginning to attract attention. In these cases the decision not to damage the career of one spouse requires geographical separation. For a description of such couples, see Ngai
(1974).

[5]Two interesting accounts of how husbands experience life with successful
career women can be found in S. M. Miller (1971) and Nadelson and
Eisenberg (1977).

[6]According to Weingarten (1974), 90% of professional women are married
to professionals, whereas the same is true for only 10% of professional
men.

[7]This sense of competence appears to occur in a wide range of situations in
which males are absent from home. Women whose husbands are away at
war typically find that the need to make decisions and to perform tasks
usually assigned to their husbands gradually builds a level of self-
confidence shaken only by their awareness of the problems they will face in
reverting to old patterns upon their husbands' return. The anthropologist
Beatrice Whiting (1977) reports a high level of self-esteem among Kenyan
women who do farming and trading, thus providing food and clothing for
their children, while husbands are employed away from home in urban

centers.
[8]Because of social pressures, many childless persons have banded together in a new support group, the National Association for Non-Parents.
[9]It is interesting that no childless woman in the sample reported a desire for only one child. Apparently women make their decision after they have had a child and find that one is sufficient.
[10]See also the report "Infant Day Care Experience" in the February 1977 newsletter of the Developmental Psychology Division, American Psychological Association.

VI. Schools and Competence

An Historical Overview

In the quest for social justice and social change it is an old American tradition to turn to schools. The tradition has been reinforced since the advent of compulsory education, which insures that almost all young people must spend many hours in the schools, vulnerable to being shaped by what happens there. Philosophers, policitians, citizens, parents, pressure groups--all have attempted to designate the schools as agents who can serve various goals:

> to mold characters, to instill patriotism, to develop civic responsibility, to assimilate newcomers to the majority culture, to provide occupational training...and to create equality (Ravitch, 1975).

Now, educational institutions are being asked to take a major responsibility for counteracting sexism and for preparing women to occupy positions of high status and influence. In consequence, as the historian David Tyack points out, educational institutions and educators are expected to be ahead of society at large, to be more free of prejudice, more enlightened in their views, in order to take the lead in undoing and remedying injustice (Tyack, 1975).

At the same time, on the other hand, the schools are viewed by many not only as potential agents of social justice but also as in part responsible for the present difficulties women face. Evidence cited for this accusation covers a wide range: the domination of block corners by boys in preschools; sexist readers in elementary schools; high-school guidance counselors who direct girls toward low-status, traditionally female occupations; universities that fail to provide role models of feminine achievement. Although schools and educators may in general be more progressive in their values than their communities or even than student peer groups, as Tyack has noted, very few educational institutions can boast about their record with respect to their female students or staff.

As late as the early 1800's, opportunities for elementary education were much more restricted for young girls than for boys. In 1805 in New London, Connecticut, for example, girls were allowed to attend the town school for the first time, but only in the summer: there would be no need for fuel, boys were busy in the fields, and women could be hired for cheap wages to teach them (Sklar, 1976).

From the founding of Harvard in 1636 to the opening of Oberlin in 1837, women were completely barred from colleges (Graham, 1975). When finally granted access, the reasons were as often to be found in economic pressures--a scarcity of male students or a need to train more teachers--as in ideology.[1] Whatever motivated the change, Tyack suggests, access to post-secondary education was one of the two "revolutions" in the history of women and education that took place in the century between 1820 and 1920.

The second revolution was the change in attitudes and beliefs about the intellect of women. In the nineteenth century experts believed, and convinced the public, that women's intelligence was inferior to that of men. Moreover, the process of studying--especially studying philosophy rather than painting--was believed to be intensely harmful to women's health, which was considered frail, and to their future reproductive and maternal functioning. It is hard nowadays to comprehend the impact of such views on young women who cared about intellectual activities. In a speech in 1907 M. Carey Thomas, president of Bryn Mawr College, recalled her early anxieties:

> I was always wondering whether it could be really true, as everyone thought, that boys were cleverer than girls. Indeed, I cared so much that I never dared ask any grownup person the direct question, not even my father or mother, because I feared to hear the reply. ...I can remember weeping over the account of Adam and Eve because it seemed to me that the curse pronounced on Eve might imperil girls' going to college...I was terror-struck lest I, and every other woman with me, were doomed to live as pathological invalids in a universe merciless to woman as a sex (1974).

She paid a special visit, she confessed, to the one college woman she could find, trembling first with fear that the woman might be a freak and then with relief that she was not.

Medical authorities on women maintained that brain and ovaries could not develop properly at the same time. In the nineteenth century medical orthodoxy proclaimed a definite consensus about the nature of women:

In males the intellectual propensities of the brain
dominated, while the female's nervous system and emotions prevailed over her conscious and rational faculties
(Smith-Rosenberg & Rosenberg, 1973).

Since woman's raison d'etre was her reproductive role, her
nature was thus as it should be. In an 1882 book, *Parturition
without Pain: A Code of Directions for Escaping the Primal
Curse,* the author, Dr. Holbrook, stated that "the Almighty
in creating the female sex, had taken the uterus and built up a
woman around it" (Smith-Rosenberg & Rosenberg, 1973).
(Lest this view be considered quaint, professors, male and
female, in at least one prestigious women's college in the
1960's, were still reminded to take certain "monthly" events
into account in assigning work to their students.)

Since advanced studies for women were likely to cause
physical deterioration, and since an adolescent girl's vital
energies had to be devoted to the development of her
reproductive organs, it followed that intellectual activities
could only damage her. This concept of limited energies,
which assumes that one activity diminishes another, is not so
different from the viewpoint of Helene Deutsch more than a
half a century later about the possible effect of intellectual activities on a woman: "Woman's intellectuality is, to a large
extent, paid for by the loss of valuable feminine qualities"
(Deutsch, 1944, p. 290).

Although secondary education was considered to be almost
as dangerous as higher education, outbursts became even
more agonized when women began to enter colleges in increasing numbers: "Women could now spend the entire
period between the beginning of menstruation and the
maturation of their ovarian systems in nerve-draining
studies" (Smith-Rosenberg & Rosenberg, 1973). Women in
colleges were often urged to take lighter course loads than
men. The Regents of the University of Wisconsin cautioned

that "education is greatly to be desired but it is better that the future matrons of the state should be without a University training than that it should be produced at the fearful expense of ruined health" (Smith-Rosenberg & Rosenberg, 1973).

Given the tenacity of many such attitudes, it is not surprising that the "revolutions" have yet to be completed. Women do not yet have equal access to higher education, nor are they consistently viewed as equally qualified for strenuous intellectual pursuits. At several points in the writing of this chapter, we have wondered whether our discussions of barriers facing women will seem outdated in the near future, given the impact of Title IX of the Education Act of 1972, (which legislates equality of opportunity within schools), the increasingly successful pressure against sexism in texts and curricula by women and other concerned groups, and the raised consciousness among educators about the importance to women of competent role models. A recent case, however, has left us shaken. In 1975, a young girl successfully sued for admission to a previously all-male public school in Philadelphia, one which was noted for its intellectual excellence. While the school continued its attempt to delay the court order for her enrollment, newspapers reported the views of those opposed. The president of the alumni association said that the admission of girls threatened the ability of the school to provide a quality education for boys, "many of whom become prominent in our society." The principal put his objections in these terms: "Our program is geared to a man-to-man relationship...our English students read Chaucer in the unexpurgated edition..in a coed class there is certain language which just could not be used" (*New York Times,* September 5, 1975).

Such views of course reflect general attitudes toward women in our society: Women neither do nor need to become "prominent"; as sexual beings their presence alongside males threatens the camaraderie and ease of the classroom. This link between women's exclusion from educational experiences and the limitations on their role in society surfaces again in General William Westmoreland's comments about the "silliness" of the recent decision to permit women to enter West Point:

> One woman in 10,000 could lead in combat but she would be a freak and we're not running the military academy for freaks...They are asking women to do impossible things. I don't believe women can carry a pack, live in a foxhole, or go a week without taking a bath (*New York Times,* June, 1, 1976).

The Impact of Educational Institutions on Feminine Competence

In analyzing the impact of educational institutions on feminine competence there are three major areas to be examined: the structure of the educational system itself--the relative position, authority, and roles of the women and men who work within its institutions; stereotyping and restrictions based upon sex; and the effect of teacher-student interactions upon girls' development.

Concern about ways in which schools discriminate against one sex is not new. Until recently, however, such concerns focused on boys; researchers addressed reasons for *boys'* underachievement and difficulties with reading. Since most teachers were women (for reasons discussed below) much of the anxiety about the fate of boys was directed toward the feminizing effects of women teachers. Although such concerns are at least a century old, they have been most recently expressed by Patricia Sexton (1969) in *The Feminized Male.* Ironically, educators have never expressed concern that girls would be masculinized by attempts to increase the number of male teachers (Tyack, 1974). And since female students were not perceived to be future achievers, any concern about *their* underachievement was rare. (At least that was true until the appearance of Sputnik and the national debate about how to produce more mathematicians and scientists.)

Only when pressure mounted to get more women into high-prestige occupations did girls' problems with achievement receive attention. A Carnegie Commission (1973) investigation of women's under-representation in graduate schools recently found, for example, that girls' school achievement (as measured by grades), though initially superior to that of boys, became lower with age until finally, by graduate school, it fell below that of males.

Structure and Status: The Position of Women in Educational Institutions

"Pedagogical harems," are what David Tyack calls the schools; the sultans, of course, are the principals and superintendents. Statistics concerning the position of women in the school system have been widely publicized recently, as more women attempt to attain positions of authority (Baden, 1975; *New York Times,* July 1, 1975). Women constitute 60% of all teachers and 80% of all elementary school teachers; yet 80% of elementary school principals and 98% of high school principals are men. Only about 1% of school superintendents are women. Thus there is an educational pyramid with women at the bottom and men at the top. The position of women is worse at present than it was in the 1940's, when 41% of elementary school principals were women, although statistics for that decade may reflect the absence of men during World War II.

What message is given to girls when most teachers are

female, and principals and superintendents are not, asks the sociologist Sara Lightfoot (1975):

> Does it seem confusing to children that the woman teacher dominates their world behind the classroom door while men (i.e., the principal, her husband) control the teacher in the outside world?

It is probably not confusing for long. Children soon sort out the difference between being in charge of children and being in charge of the world. As a girl advances and enters college and graduate school, she sees, once again, that senior professors are mostly males, although women may be instructors, lecturers, or laboratory assistants.

Indeed a decline in the percentage of women in college faculties has been occurring. In 1918, 70% of the faculty of women's colleges were female, as were 18% of the faculty of coeducational institutions. In 1970, the women's colleges had less than 50% women faculty; coeducational colleges had 14%. Even by 1975, the percentage of women on colleges and university faculties had risen barely above 21% (Graham, 1975).

For historical perspective on forces affecting women teachers in grammar schools, we must trace changes in the educational system in America during the fifty years from 1870 to 1920 (Tyack, 1974). A rapid increase in school attendance and a labor-short economy combined to create a need for teachers who would work in subordinate positions for long hours and little pay. Women, specifically unmarried women, seemed custom-made for such positions. It was (and is still) believed that women had a special understanding of children, partly because of what was perceived as their own childlike nature. Women were explicitly praised for having the attitudes considered appropriate for teachers: in 1841, the Boston School Committee officially congratulated women teachers for their acquiescent demeanor. In the 1860's, the National Educational Association did not permit full membership to women; they had to sit in the galleries at meetings and could not address the gathering. Concurrently, the percentage of women grammar school teachers rose rapidly, from 59% in 1870 to 86% in 1920.

Another educational arena in which the position of women has in turn advanced and retreated is in the women's colleges, which often were founded in a feminist spirit. Most such fervor was short-lived. M. Carey Thomas is perhaps the most prominent example of feminist motivation in her vision for Bryn Mawr, yet in the 1960's the college was accused by students of betraying her ideals (Schneider, 1974). Smith College has recently been found guilty of sex descrimination in faculty hiring; in 1972 only 32% of the faculty were women, compared with 58% in 1958. During the past 35 years, only 13 of 23 presidents of the "Seven Sister" colleges have been women (Graham, 1975). Perhaps for the same reasons that the prestige of an occupation or social role decreases if it is associated with women, the prestige of a college slowly but inevitably has come to be linked to the presence of men--if not male students, then at least male faculty and a male president. One woman scholar has confessed publicly to this view:

> The president of one highly rated women's college stated proudly in the early 1960's that at last he had managed to increase the proportion of men faculty to half the total. And I, in tune with those times of unraised consciousness, congratulated him on this proof that the college could attract the best scholar-teachers, implying that meant men (Tidball, 1973).

But times are changing. When a man was recently appointed to be President of Bryn Mawr College, one alumna protested in outrage that the clear implication was that the college had not produced one female capable of being its president (Schneider, 1974). Understanding of this implication has led more women's colleges to seek women presidents.

But to search is not always to find. As is so often the case, internal and external barriers combine to keep the number of women administrators low. Partly because most such positions have been barred to them, women have been as reluctant to prepare for and to seek high positions in educational institutions as in other fields. Moreover, an elementary or high school teacher may become aware of a vacancy in the position of principal, yet decide against applying. One such teacher was quoted as saying, "No, for two good reasons-- July and August" (*New York Times,* July 13, 1975). She might have also answered, "And nights, weekends, and holidays." Like many top executive positions, educational administration has been defined and structured to include endless hours of work per week. Many women, out of a genuine concern for family needs, avoid such responsibilities. In her analysis of past presidents of the Seven Sister schools, significantly enough, Patricia Graham (1975) found that only two of the thirteen women were married at the time of their appointment.

The problem of family responsibilities does not, however, account fully for the degree of male domination in the upper levels of the educational pyramid. In her 1975 analysis of school systems in the metropolitan Boston area, Ruth Baden found neither interest nor concern among school administrators with the absence of women from their ranks. The process of choosing principals and superintendents is revealing: although the process is nominally open at the beginning--positions are advertised--it ends with personal recommendations by (male) superintendents and their staff. One personnel official told Baden, "Actually we have a pretty good idea of who would make a 'good' principal and we try to provide these people with leadership opportunities." There seemed no awareness that the resulting all-male administration should be a cause for concern. When Baden mentioned the problem of women having no power, the administrator she was interviewing corrected her. "He told me it was only my singular view of 'power' which caused me to interpret the picture as I did. 'This school system doesn't view principals and heads of departments as more powerful than teachers.' " There are clear echoes here of the "hand that rocks the cradle" philosophy.

It is true that until recently systems open to women administrators did not find many candidates. In the past, few women enrolled in doctoral programs in educational administration; to enroll presupposes a perception of oneself as a person who is, or can be, appropriately efficient, authoritative, assertive--a leader of men as well as women. A teacher who was asked by Baden if she had ever thought of becoming a principal, answered:

> I couldn't expose myself like that--or balance a budget--
> or do the things a principal has to do. I like to make
> waves, but when it comes to a confrontation, I hide
> behind the principal.

It would be tragic if women who delight in the role of teacher--who chose it because it fitted their needs and talents, not because it was one of the few occupations open to women--were to feel inferior by remaining there. But until present prejudices are removed, being a woman teacher will not imply free choice of that role. And at present, prejudice remains. School boards, which appoint superintendents, include few women; and the women who do serve on them are likely to be as conservative about women as the men. Boards of education are "run like the board of directors of any big corporation--by men "(*New York Times*, April 15, 1975). A survey of school superintendents confirmed that they prefer men as school board members, although some wanted the kind of women "who know when to keep their mouths shut" (*Idem*). To hire a woman superintendent is thus asking for trouble with conservative elements in the community, as one woman administrator was told when turned down for a position for which she was acknowledged to be the best qualified candidate. To fit in, one must be part of the old-boy network, a protege of already established sponsors, a person who can attend Rotary meetings and boost the schools by ingratiating himself with local male politicians (Tyack, 1975).

Patricia Schmuck (1975) interviewed ten men and thirty women administrators in the Oregon public school system. In explaining their reluctance to hire women, the men cited the need to work closely with other administrators:

> It's easier to work without women. Principals and superintendents are a management team...We need each other for survival...I wonder if we could hang together so well if some of us were women. Could she protect my job as well as her own? I don't have that concern with a guy; he talks the same language.

Similarly, a school superintendent in Utah asserted to a reporter that:

> aside from the woman who ran his lunch program, he was opposed to women administrators. Not only does no one want to work for a woman, but "Productivity in

the school business is much better when males run the operation than when women do" (*Peer Perspective,* 1975, 1).

As is often the case when widespread assumptions are studied objectively, they turn out to be debatable. A recent national research project on elementary school principals found both that students learned more and that teachers performed better in schools with women principals. Contrary to the view that no one wants to work for a woman, no differences in teacher morale were associated with the sex of the principal. Women principals, perhaps because of the bias against them, were older and more experienced than the men; in fact 34% of the male principals had *never* taught in elementary schools, compared with only 3% of the women. This difference may well account for the findings. The authors comment:

> Our findings undercut the arguments generally used to support the male preference policy in selecting elementary school principals...One of its unanticipated and unrecognized educational consequences has been that the learning of pupils and the quality of performance of teachers has been adversely affected(Gross & Trask, 1976, p.20).

This study may well serve to accelerate the changes already taking place as women begin to enroll in school administration programs.

The Question of Co-education

The question of single-sex (here, all-female) versus co-educational institutions is another variable in the educational structure with implications for feminine competence. It has

been part of American progressive thought that all segregation is bad, whether that of the sexes or the races. Usually, indeed, underlying the pressure for integration is the assumption of unequal status of the two groups involved: the less
dominant group is seen as likely to benefit from being in-
tegrated into the more dominant group. Thus segregation is
understood, often rightly, as an attempt to keep the less
favored group from certain advantages.

Because segregation is so contrary to our ideology, its
benefits under certain circumstances have tended either to go
unnoticed or to be violently attacked. Now, however, the
findings concerned with women are being scrutinized more
objectively--perhaps because women have begun to question
whether what is all-female is necessarily second-class. In
1975, applications to and enrollments in women's colleges,
according to *Time* magazine, were at their highest in many
years. Patricia Graham (1975) points out that one commmon
characteristic of many successful women is attendance at all-
girl high schools and/or colleges. There, she suspects, they
may have received more encouragement from teachers whose
concern was not concentrated on male students. The analogy
to the daughter in a family with no male siblings is clear.

The necessity for role models for competent women has of
course become almost a cliche. Elizabeth Tidball (1973), who
examined the records of 1500 women achievers listed in
Who's Who in American Women, found that significantly
more had attended all-female rather than co-educational colleges. The crucial variable, according to further analysis, was
the proportion of women faculty, while the total number of
men in the college environment was negatively related to
women's later achievement.

Thus, at present, data indicate that the impact of coeducation on women's achievement is negative. Yet the current trend is toward increasing numbers of mergers of single-
sex institutions, even while some famous women's colleges

resist the pressure. Susan Lloyd (in press) is studying the history of one all-girls' private secondary school, Abbot Academy, recently merged with Phillips Andover Academy. Although such merger decisions are often painful, economic factors tend to make them mandatory for the women's school, while the men's school seeks to attract the many excellent prospective students in search of co-educational experiences. At Abbot a sense of loss was shared by many among both the faculty and the students, who felt deprived of the sense of community they had had and who faced the problem of coping with masculine domination and rejection. Opponents of their point of view are convinced that women must learn early to deal with the real world (which of course includes men and negative male attitudes) and to test themselves against the full range of talent. They also doubt that women must be segregated in order to experience the benefits of faculty encouragement, opportunities for leadership, and role models.

One apparently salient finding must be carefully weighed. When the mini-society that is a school consists of all females, it appears that the idea of what is feminine expands to include such items as high office, science, athletics, top grades, whereas the idea of what is not feminine contracts. One of the most intriguing aspects of the motive to avoid success (defined in Chapter 7) is that it is rare in girls attending all-girl rather than co-educational high schools and/or elementary schools. Girls in co-educational high schools, according to Winchell, Fenner and Shaver (1974), showed significantly more fear of success than those in all-girl high schools, and no girl presently in co-educational high school who had attended an all-girl elementary school showed such fears. Early attendance at an all-girl school can seemingly provide some degree of "immunity" from the forces that create ambivalence toward success. Perhaps non-stereotyped behavior there becomes frequent, rewarding, and hence habit-forming and self-perpetuating.

Sex-Role Stereotyping

In its broadest sense, stereotyping includes all the forms of restrictiveness based on sex that exist within schools: images, ideas, and policies concerning females (and males) as they are reflected in courses, athletics, counseling, etc. From the absence of women in history texts and shop courses, to the explicit or subtle guidance toward choosing nursing rather than medicine, girls are exposed to experiences that limit rather than expand their competence. Such restrictions are often based not only on traditional views of the nature of women but on the concern of educators that personality development and solid "sexual identity" (which is rarely clearly defined) depend on maintaining some sort of distinction between the sexes.

The earliest effective investigations of stereotyping and its harmfulness came from feminist groups such as the Task Force on Women in Words and Images, of the National Organization for Women. Their research, reported in "Dick and Jane as Victims," examined elementary readers, in which they found girls portrayed less often than boys, tending to be minor characters or onlookers, and showing fear and passivity much more often than independence and assertiveness. Pictures of mothers would leave one to infer that they were born wearing aprons and with babies affixed to their arms. In social studies curricula, the experiences and contributions of women were almost completely ignored.

Discoveries of innumerable areas of stereotyping followed rapidly. A major article published in 1973 in the *Harvard Educational Review* revealed extensive, pervasive, and denigrating assumptions about women--not only in readers but in curriculum requirements and educational testing (Saario, Jacklin, & Tittle, 1973). Even items on achievement tests express stereotypic, harmful assumptions that escape, but permeate, the consciousness: "In the United States voters do not directly choose the man they wish to be president.''

Vocational interest tests have, until recently, been notoriously biased in items and scoring, and therefore in impact (Tittle, 1974). Guidance counselors for their part have done little to counter the stereotypes and the limited aspirations that girls bring to, as well as acquire in, school. Notice, for instance, that although teaching can rarely be a part-time occupation, while medicine is well-suited to such arrangements, the myth persists that being a teacher somehow is more compatible with being a mother. Whether because of realistic concern about the barriers girls would encounter or because of assumptions about the negative effect on mental health of choosing ''masculine'' occupations, guidance counselors have in the past rarely challenged restrictions or fought stereotypes. In their views about femininity, indeed, counselors themselves are no different from other people. In one study, counselors were shown tapes of interviews with two girls who had supposedly made deviant (engineering) or traditional (home economics) career choices. The girls were asked about themselves and their families, and the counselors were asked to rate the appropriateness of the choices, their own liking for each girl, and the degree to which the girl was in need of counseling. While both girls were equally liked, the conforming girl was seen as making more appropriate choices, and the deviant girl as more in need of counseling (Thomas & Stewart, 1971).

Patterns of Teachers' Interactions with Girls

Until recently the unstated and untested assumption of many researchers and educators was that boys had a particularly difficult time in the classroom, but that girls' experiences were more positive and enhancing. This assumption rested on the congruence between the image of the ideal girl--

passive, dutiful, orderly--and the image of the ideal student, at least in elementary school. A further postulate was that the teacher, also being female and probably also passive, dutiful, and orderly, would prefer female students.

Some research does support these assumptions. In one study (Levitin & Chananie, 1972), the liking of elementary-school teachers for, and their approval of, different types of male and female students were measured, using written descriptions of fictitious people. No particular pattern of approval turned up, but with respect to liking, teachers preferred students described as achievers over non-achievers and dependent over independent. Of those students who were both achievers and dependent, girls were liked better than boys, dependent girls best of all--a finding interpreted as reflecting the fact that achievement and dependency are expected in the classroom and are sex-appropriate for girls. Thus girls with these characteristics were favored and almost guaranteed teacher liking. In another study (Feshbach, 1969), the least-liked student was the independent, assertive girl; because both independence and assertiveness were considered inappropriate for girls, such students were disliked.

The propensity of teachers to prefer that girls behave in ways resembling the feminine sex-role stereotype was also documented in a series of studies by Fagot and her colleagues (Fagot, 1975; Fagot & Patterson, 1969). Teachers tended to reward sex-typed behavior associated with the feminine role, whether the behavior was shown by boys or girls. The studies did not, however, find evidence that teachers' patterns had any effects at all; that is, boys taught by women showed no more feminine behavior at the end than at the beginning of the school year. The impact of teacher patterns is thus unclear; moreover, existing student behavior cannot necessarily be ascribed to teacher behavior. One observer who set out to detect teachers' influence on sex-role stereotyping in preschools found that she could pick up little in the behavior of teachers to account for the extremely stereotyped behavior of the children--their avoidance of the opposite sex, among other things (Joffee, 1974). Influences other than the school, she concluded, must be at work.

That boys receive more attention, both positive (praise) and negative (criticism) than girls, researchers seem to agree; and they receive this attention whether or not they are physically close to the teacher (Brophy & Goode, 1974). Girls, on the other hand, tend to get attention only when they are near the teacher, thus encouraging proximity and dependence behaviors. Girls may indeed come to feel ineffective in controlling their environment, one researcher suggests, because when they seek attention they are often ignored unless they are close to the teacher (Serbin, 1974). A thoughtful preschool teacher recently commented to us that she had to remind herself to sit down and get involved with pairs of girls talking or playing quietly rather than reserve her attention for disruptive, noisier boys. Although boys are in fact somewhat more disruptive, researchers have found that this difference does not account for the greater surveillance or attention they receive (Maccoby & Jacklin, 1974).

The studies just described were based upon observations, usually in preschools or elementary schools, by researchers who first observed and then speculated about the meaning of what they saw. In a different approach, secondary-school teachers were asked directly about their sex-role attitudes and preferences (Ricks & Pyke, 1973). The teachers believed, in the first place, that there were differences between the sexes that made it advisable to treat boys and girls differently, and beyond that, that students wanted differential treatment. They believed that boys want and need to be treated more sternly than girls. Despite the findings cited above about the preference of *elementary school* teachers for feminine, docile traits, this sample of *secondary-school* teachers much preferred working with male rather than female students, on the ground that boys were more active in exchanging ideas. The few who preferred girls almost always referred to the ease of discipline. Perhaps the greater importance of subject matter in secondary education accounts for the differences between these teachers and those in elementary schools.

In the Ricks and Pyke study, teachers thought students preferred male teachers, although only 17% thought female teachers were actually less effective than males. This finding is borne out by the work of Jessie Bernard (1966), who found that when a male and a female lecturer were trained to give the same lecture in the same manner, students saw the male as expressing real "facts," while the female was to them only giving her opinions.

Because women students have been under-represented in graduate schools, investigators have sought in college classrooms for patterns that might account for women feeling less able and willing to consider and apply for graduate programs. Whether female undergraduates received less encouragement, attention, and feedback from their professors than did males was the subject of one study (Sternglanz & Lyberger-Ficek, 1977). Observations in the classroom showed that professors, whether male or female, responded as readily to female as to male students with respect to answering their questions, encouraging discussion, and engaging in interchanges. Female students, however, were less likely than male to respond when professors attempted to initiate an interaction, and they themselves initiated fewer interactions than did males. These latter findings were less pronounced in classes with female professors, perhaps because female teachers tend to be less authoritarian and demanding. Yet the female students preferred male teachers and were thus caught in a destructive cycle operating against their best interests.

Interventions: How Schools Can Help Women

A wide variety of proposals has been made about how to improve the impact of schools on feminine competence, suggestions ranging from providing carpentry for pre-school girls to providing day-care for children of women professors. To increase the number of women in influential positions, what is required in the field of education is not very different from what is required in other occupations. With respect to girls and women as students, however, schools and educators have a special role, and the school setting offers a focused arena for efforts toward intervention.

One major goal has been to provide curriculum materials that portray women in non-traditional ways, direct attention to the importance of their contributions, and stimulate the students to examine and re-think their own stereotypes. On the pre-school level, Barbara Sprung (1974) has described the process of change as it took place in one school. She followed in detail the concerns and efforts of parents as well as teachers, and the anxieties both felt about attempting to change sex-role images. Going beyond the usual suggestions of encouraging doll-play for boys and block-building for girls, she emphasizes the importance of exposing children to varieties of family structure and occupational roles; for example, children visited a woman architect while she was supervising a building project on site.

Going one step up the educational ladder, Barbara Harrison (1974) has described the process by which parents and staff in an elementary school united in an effort to root out sexism. Although the school was a private, progressive institution that prided itself on success in undoing racism, many of the adults expressed concern about the possibility of creating confusion in sex roles and about the morality of imposing feminist views on children who were supposed to learn to make their own moral judgments. Gradually, however, the parents became convinced of the damage the traditional stereotypes were inflicting on girls; once they were persuaded, they in turn convinced the teachers and helped them to change. Many subtle, almost subliminal forms of impoverishment came to light--such as the fact that some teachers thought it was "cute" when girls were teased by boys.

Do intervention programs have detectable, significant effects? To answer that question, one such program scheduled a before-and-after analysis of effects. Marcia Guttentag and her colleagues (Guttentag & Bray 1976) provided teachers in several suburban kindergarten, 5th- and 9th-grade classrooms with detailed curricula--books, information units, guides for discussion. Teachers attended workshops that included presentations on the effects of sexism.Goals of the program, tailored to grade level, were clearly delineated. All students were encouraged to become less stereotyped in their play and interests; to see adults in more varied roles; and to consider a wider range of occupations. Older children were expected to become more aware of and critical of stereotyping around them. Effects were assessed by before-and-after measures both of sex-role stereotyping and of patterns of classroom interaction. To measure stereotyping, as one example, students were shown pictures of males and females in traditional and non-traditional roles and then asked to make up a story about the pictures. As to interaction patterns, the hypotheses were that girls would receive more praise and criticism after the intervention and that girls would increase their activity in terms of initiating and contributing to classroom interactions. Contrary to expectation, however, no such changes emerged; though other results were somewhat more positive. Girls did become significantly less stereotyped, along with kindergarten boys. But 5th-grade boys did not change, and 9th-grade boys become even more stereotyped.

To interpret the effect on 9th-grade boys we need to turn back to the discussion of the "sexism" in preschoolers that was seemingly unrelated to teacher behavior and attitudes. At certain critical ages, it seems, children may intensify their efforts to construct and to maintain definite and rigid sex roles. Both preschoolers (who are attempting to grasp the concept of sexual identity) and adolescents (who are coming to terms with heterosexuality) may be particularly vulnerable to rigid thinking and at least temporarily, extremely resistant to change. Nursery school teachers, "liberated" mothers and fathers of adolescent girls, and researchers all report their frustration and puzzlement over inexplicably stereotyped behavior and attitudes; they wonder what they could be doing "wrong." It is important, therefore, to establish whether there in fact are such critical ages, what their function may be, and what processes govern the outcome.

A recent study is relevant here (Drabman, Hammer, & Jarvie). Children in 1st-, 4th-, and 7th-grade classes were shown a videotape of a young boy's visit to his pediatrician, a woman. A male nurse greeted the boy. The names of each were repeated several times during the film: Dr. Mary Nancy and Nurse David Gregory. Yet when questioned afterwards, all but one first grader picked a masculine name for the doctor, and all picked a feminine name for the nurse. Results for the fourth graders were similar. Among 7th graders, however, only about 10% gave the wrong answer.

If younger children, then, are not influenced by occasional exceptions to societal norms, they may also be immune to attempts by teachers to transmit images contradictory to the realities around them. Thus the burden of change ultimately rests on society rather than on the schools. In any case, we must not restrict intervention efforts to young people. For women who have led traditional lives, most observers agree, a critical time for reviewing the past and assessing the future-- including possible new beginnings--is in early middle age, when family responsibilities lessen and need is felt for alternate bases for identity and self-esteem. Many post-secondary institutions are now beginning to meet the needs of those women through continuing education programs that offer support and flexibility both in programs and in credit for past courses and life experiences.

Women who have participated in such programs report not only academic gains but great psychological benefits, including increased self-awareness, self-esteem and self-confidence (Astin, 1976). The experience of being part of an educational program along with other women with similar concerns and goals seems to be a crucial ingredient in the process of developing new skills and venturing into new arenas.

Notes

[1] For an historical account of influences on the admission of women to medical schools, see Walsh (1977).

VII. Achievement: Attitudes, Beliefs, Motives

"Whenever I beat a boy in sports, I lose a boyfriend," a young girl complained recently to an advice-to-teenagers columnist. The adviser, known for her liberated views about adolescent *sexual* behavior, replied to this question about *achievement* behavior by warning that although there was nothing wrong with winning, the girl should realize that a boy cannot be both a competitor and a romantic figure.

Such messages inevitably color a girl's attitudes and beliefs with respect to achievement. Indeed, for most women such messages have been multiplied many times over in the course of their socialization. Given the many reasons for women's failure to fulfill their potential, Lois Hoffman (1972) argues, "one is almost tempted to ask why women achieve at all."

In this chapter we shall examine research concerning women's motives and beliefs relevant to achievement. We shall give particular attention to how they perceive the causes of their successes and failures--to what psychologists call attribution patterns. We are handicapped by a paucity of information about adult women; most studies have been carried out with students in elementary school through college. Nevertheless, we shall be able to trace some of the sources and consequences of typical female patterns and to indicate fruitful intervention points for altering them. We begin with some background data on women and the occupational structure.

Occupational Attainments

The pace of women's entry into the labor force in the mid-70's has been labeled "extraordinary" by Alan Greenspan, former chairman of the President's Council of Economic Advisors, and "the single most outstanding phenomenon of our century" by economist Eli Ginzburg (*New York Times,* September 12, 1976). Nevertheless, the relative status of women's work, compared with men's, has not yet changed radically for the better.

One would expect an increase in the percentages of women in high-status occupations. Entering classes of law and medical schools are now typically one-quarter to one-third women, and a 1975 survey of women entering college disclosed that 16.9% planned such careers as lawyer, physician, engineer, or business executive, compared with only 5.9% a decade earlier *(New York Times,* September 10, 1976). In spite of all this, however, the overwhelming majority of working women will continue to hold low-level, routine jobs. And in our review of research on the relative occupational aspirations and expectations of males and females (Barnett & Baruch, 1976), we found a consistent and distressing picture:

1. Girls choose a more restricted, less varied range of occupations than do boys.

2. Occupational choices are highly stereotyped with respect to sex from a very early age.

3. About one-half to two-thirds of school-age girls aspire to be either a teacher, nurse, or secretary, regardless of their social class or race. Because these occupations are of moderate rather than low social status, and because very young boys often choose to be policemen and firemen, young girls' aspirations are high relative to boys. By the end of high school, however, girls' choices are unchanged; boys' have gone up and surpass those of girls.

4. There is evidence that girls specifically and intentionally avoid high-prestige occupations. Rosalind Barnett (1975) asked boys and girls aged seven to seventeen to rank their most and least preferred occupations. The prestige ratings of these occupations were analyzed in relation to the preferences. For boys, the prestige of an occupation was a positive influence: the higher the prestige, the more they preferred the enter the occupation. For girls, prestige was a negative influence: the higher the prestige of an occupation, the more they expressed an aversion to entering it.

Soon many of these findings may be outdated; as the occupational structure changes with respect to women's representation in high-status occupations, children's plans and goals should reflect the shift. Nevertheless, research on many facets of women's achievement still reveals attitudinal and motivational patterns that tend to impair women's functioning. Among the earliest such research was that on achievement motivation.

The Achievement Motive

The concept of motive concerns behavior directed towards a goal. Because the person who is "motivated" shows persistence in seeking the goal, the intensity of a motive is often inferred from the person's flexibility and determination in overcoming obstacles and finding paths to its accomplishment. Motives are also usually spoken of as stable tendencies, either innate or shaped early in life. The motive to achieve, conceptualized by pioneer researchers David McClelland and J. W. Atkinson (McClelland, Atkinson, Clark, & Lowell, 1976) as striving to achieve standards of excellence, was considered to originate in the child's early desire for love and approval. At first parents provide these rewards in return for good behavior and performance. Gradually, however, the child also rewards herself by feeling good when meeting her now internal standards of performance.

In their early studies of achievement motivation, Atkinson and McClelland attempted to arouse the motive by various techniques, one of which was deprivation--leading subjects to believe they had performed poorly on an intelligence test. They were then given the Thematic Apperception Test, in which one writes stories in response to visual cues; the strength of the achievement motive could be determined by analyzing the stories for achievement-related imagery. This formulation focused on the achievement motive as a stable characteristic of individual personalities.

More recently, attention has turned to other determinants of achievement motivation, particularly those arising from the characteristics of particular situations. Such factors as a person's expectancies about the chances and consequences of success (or failure), as well as the importance of those consequences, must be known in order to predict how that person will behave in each achievement situation (Atkinson &

Feather, 1966). Consider the girl who requested advice about her athletic achievements. If romantic attention from her male partner is what she values, and if she expects to forfeit it by beating him at tennis, her motivation to achieve in this particular situation may well be inhibited--even (or especially) if she estimates her chances of winning to be excellent. Our prediction about her performance (after she receives advice from the columnist) is that she will lose; yet it would be wrong to assume that striving to achieve standards of excellence is not part of her personality. This "expectancy-value theory" of motivation provides a conceptual framework for understanding the complex interaction of various motives and beliefs in the determination of performance in achievement-oriented activities.

As is so often the case, the earliest studies of achievement motivation were carried out with male subjects. As soon as females were studied, it became apparent that theories and findings based on studies of men could not be assumed to apply to women. Two major problems required explanation, as stated by Stein and Bailey (1973): (a) techniques of arousing achievement motivation used successfully with men, e.g., leading them to believe they had performed poorly on an intelligence test, did not have the predicted effect on women; and (b) achievement motivation scores did not have the predicted relationship to actual performance. Women, moreover, typically set lower levels of aspirations for performance for themselves than did men, and expected to achieve lower levels of performance. Both aspirations and expectations were often unrealistically low.[1]

An advance in understanding women's achievement motivation came from Matina Horner (1968). She set forth a motive for the avoidance of success, the fear that negative social consequences will accompany success in competive situations. Working in the context of the expectancy-value theory of motivation, she argued that for many women, the "psychological meaning" of success is that it will entail social rejection and loss of femininity. Thus fear of success may act as a potential and formidable psychological barrier to actual achievement. On the assumption that the apprehension arises from traditional sex-role standards, it can lead women to expect "that they can be unsexed by success" (Horner, 1972). It also followed, according to Horner's hypothesis, that ambivalence toward achievement would be more characteristic of women than of men and would impair their task performance, particularly when they had to compete with men.

Using the methodology developed by McClelland and his colleagues, she asked able college students to write stories to a verbal cue: for women, "At the end of first-term finals, Anne finds herself at the top of her medical school class;" for male subjects, the principal character was "John" rather than "Anne." More than 65% of the women, but less than 10% of the men, wrote stories reflecting fear of success. Such stories typically were negative toward "Anne," and described the undesirable consequences of her success, or they were bizarre, indicating anxiety or denial.

> Anne has a boyfriend, Carl, in the same class, and they are quite serious. Anne met Carl at college, and they started dating about their sophomore year in undergraduate school. Anne is rather upset and so is Carl. She wants him to be higher scholastically than she is. Anne will deliberately lower her academic standing the next term, while she does all she subtly can to help Carl. His grades come up and Anne soon drops out of med school. They marry and he goes on in school while she raises their family.

> She is in a class of a great number of highly intelligent and competitive people, one of whom is her fiance ...Anne is ambitious and has more innate ability than

> does her boyfriend. Anne is fearful that this situation will have a detrimental effect on their relationship and later on their marriage. Her superiority will mean that her eventual earning power will be greater. Although he would never let her know, her husband would resent that. It is important that Anne marrry this man because of their closeness. But Anne will *never be entirely happy* in the marriage because she must always hold back her mentality and vocational desires.
>
> Anne is talking to her counselor. The counselor says she will make a fine nurse. She will continue her med school courses. She will study very hard and find she can and will become a good nurse.

Perhaps the most important finding was that those women who feared success, as indicated by the stories they wrote, performed significantly more poorly on tasks (anagrams) in mixed-sex competitive situations than when they worked alone. Women who did not fear success did not show this pattern, nor did most men. What comes out of Horner's study, therefore, is the possibility that many able women, for whom successful achievement was an attainable goal, did expect negative consequences from success, and when competing with men did inhibit their performance accordingly.

To be both successful and anxious is of course perfectly possible; detecting anxiety in an individual need not predict certain failure. Nevertheless, Horner's concept, offering as it did a possible explanation of women's unequal occupational attainment (Tresemer, 1976), generated much interest. Subsequent studies have attempted to replicate and expand her findings.[2] Of special interest are recent findings that men are as likely as women to write stories exhibiting fear of success; perhaps there may have been an increase since 1964 in the proportion of men with negative attitudes toward success.

This pattern was found by Nancy Romer (1975) in a study of children in grades 5, 7-9, and 11, as well as in a replication of Horner's work using students in the same university (Hoffman, 1974c). Various interpretations are offered for this new phenomenon of male ambivalence toward success: rejection of materialism and conventional goals; a desire for careers that do not interfere with family life; and a "sour-grapes" effect--fears of men about their ability to succeed and a consequent denigration of success.

The few studies that have attempted to repeat the link between fear-of-success imagery and actual task performance have failed to do so. Neither Romer nor Hoffman found such a relationship.[3] This circumstance does not, of course, prove that girls do not inhibit their task performance in mixed-sex situations--only that one cannot predict this behavior from the stories they write. Morgan and Mauser (1972), for instance, although they found fear-of-success imagery in high-school students to be unrelated to task behavior, nevertheless also discovered that able girls, when paired with less able boys, tended to perform more poorly than when they worked alone.

As one can see, therefore, concern about negative male reactions seems to be a major inhibiting factor for females. To carry the investigation a step further, researchers have interested themselves in the question: how realistic are such fears? Do men indeed reject competent women?

In a series of studies by Steinmann and her colleagues (Steinmann & Fox, 1966), the men consistently portrayed their "ideal" woman as much more assertive than women had expected; in short, women appeared to be misinformed about men's preference for clinging-vine types. In another attempt to answer this question, Spence and Helmreich (1972) showed groups of subjects video-taped interviews of a young woman applying for the job of freshman adviser. In the film she was variously presented as having either masculine or feminine interest, and as either competent or incompetent. Male subjects liked her best when she was masculine and competent; they liked her least when she was masculine and incompetent.

Laboratory studies do not tell us about real-life situations, of course. Davis and Spiegler (1974) sought to simulate these in order to determine whether being "bright and ambitious" was the "kiss of death" for women. To this end they led subjects to believe they were selecting a partner for either an intellectual task (a team competition) or a social event (having coffee). Although both male and female subjects preferred bright partners for the intellectual tasks, the results for the social events were not as clear-cut. Men preferred bright women but women did not; however, neither pattern was statistically significant.

Even such "realistic" studies can tell us little about what happens when a man and a woman who are emotionally involved with each other face issues of competition, success, and failure. In one study, Letitia Peplau (1973) found that, as least for women rated high in motive to avoid success, competition against a boyfriend did tend to impair their task performance.

Attributions

During a recent political campaign, one unsuccessful candidate was asked to what he attributed his failure to win the local primary. He had not put sufficient effort into his campaign, he answered; he had devoted too little time and money to it. Had he tried harder, he would have won--perhaps next time! Let us imagine another unsuccessful political candidate, however, who in a series of primary campaigns, attributes losses (failure) to a lack of ability, and winning (success) to luck--perhaps the exposure of an opponent's alcoholism. Such a candidate is not likely to feel proud of winning and may well even feel ashamed of losing. And if success is a fluke, he will have little reason to keep trying.

Answer to questions such as "To what do you attribute your failures or your successes?" are the raw material with which attribution theorists deal. Attribution theory itself grew out of research on achievement-related attitudes and behavior. Atkinson (1964) defined achievement motivation, as we have seen, as "the capacity for experiencing pride in achievement," a statement interpreted by Weiner and his colleagues (Weiner, Frieze, Kukla, Reed, Rose & Rosenbaum, 1971) as the "capacity for perceiving success as caused by internal factors, particularly effort." With such a perception, one can take credit for one's successes, derive self-esteem and gratification from them, and expect future successes.

If we told attribution theorists that one of the two political candidates just described was a woman, most would guess that she was the second. When failure occurs, women are the ones who tend to believe their *abilities* inadequate, men to believe their *efforts* insufficient. When success occurs, on the other hand, women tend to think that the task must have been easy, or that luck was with them; men credit their own abilities. Using these most common of the attributions people make--effort, ability, luck, ease of task--Weiner and his co-workers constructed a two-dimensional model: internal versus external; and stable versus unstable. Ability, according to such a scheme, is both internal and stable; success attributed to ability is expected to be repeated, as is failure due to its lack. Effort, which is internal but unstable--one can always try harder--permits an individual to take credit for success and to expect to overcome failure. Luck is both external and unstable; success and failure due to luck are equally unlikely to be repeated.

Clearly the best way to build self-esteem and a sense of competence is to attribute one's successes to internal, stable factors, and one's failures to external, unstable ones. This pattern is less typical of women than men, impairing women's pride in their accomplishments (Frieze, 1975). With aspirations and expectations lowered by the consequent self-denigration, a destructive cycle is set up that is difficult to interrupt.

Not only a woman herself but those observing her success or failure, may utilize such patterns, as was found in a study whose sub-title reveals the findings: "What's skill for the male is luck for the female" (Deaux & Emswiller, 1974). A real-life example of such attributions by others appears in a male newspaper reporter's interview with Juanita Kreps, President Carter's Secretary of Commerce. The interviewer began by commenting that Secretary Kreps had been lucky in her career. The Secretary's attributions were different. "First of all," she said, "it was not luck." (*New York Sunday Times,* May 8, 1977).

It appears, according to a recent analysis, that early in life a pattern is set down in which adults' low expectancies for girls' success may lead to: less persistance at tasks; lower quality of performance; less pride in success; and more shame at failure (Parsons, Ruble, Hodges, & Small, 1976). Although the origins of this pattern are not yet well understood, the authors suggest at least three possible processes: parents and teachers may have lower expectations for girls' performance; they may provide girls with different explanations (attributions) for their successes and failures; and they may respond in different ways to the achievements of boys and girls. That parents and teachers ought to be aware of and to monitor the expectations and attributions they convey emerges as an implication of the analysis.

With respect to schools, Carol Dweck (1975) has been analyzing the experiences of young children with their

teachers in order to discover any sex differences in attributions, and ultimately to intervene where necessary. Because
girls typically behave more diligently in the classroom than do
boys, she believes, teachers tend to assume that a girl is
always trying hard and that any failures are therefore due to
her lack of ability. Boys, who appear less diligent, are likely
to be told to try harder when they fail. Thus girls may not be
receiving from teachers the message that if you try harder,
you will succeed.

Expanding the Scope of Feminine Competence

The attitudes and motives, anxieties and beliefs described
above have been potent factors in blocking the acquisition
and exercise of competence. In numerous ways women are
now moving toward a freer choice of channels for their competence. For such a change a necessary foundation is the acceptance of traits like assertiveness and competence as a
legitimate part of the self. Relevant here are attempts to
reverse the exclusion of and avoidance by women of two
previously male-dominated arenas of competence--athletics
and mathematics.

Athletic Competence

Anne C. Scott (1974) begins her article on women and
sports with a quotation from Aristotle's *Physiognomics:*

> The author of nature gave man strength of body and in-
> trepidity of mind to enable him to face great hardships,
> and to woman was given a weak and delicate constitu-
> tion, accompanied by a natural softness and modest
> timidity, which fit her for sedentary life.

Aristotelian images of masculinity and femininity die hard; from the opposition to girls playing in the Little League to discrimination against women athletes, adherence is still tenacious. According to Marie Hart (1971), the roles of woman and successful athlete in the United States are well-nigh incompatible. The powerful tradition by which sports are "an agent of masculine orientation," an initiation rite that makes men out of boys, has one of its most famous expressions in the attribution of British imperial success to the playing fields of Eton (Duke of Wellington, quoted by Oglesby, 1976). Serious athletic pursuits have been looked upon as too aggressive, "too demanding and dangerous" for girls, as socially and physically inappropriate (Frieze, McHugh & Duquin, 1976). The most controversial part of Title IX of the Educational Amendment Act of 1972, the act which forbids discrimination on the basis of sex in educational institutions receiving federal aid, is the set of guidelines for achieving equal opportunity in sports. The passion of the ensuing debates bears witness to the centrality of athletic competence in definitions of masculinity.

Feminists who protest the damaging effects of the "denial to woman of her physical powers" (Scott, 1974) point out that independence, pride, and even safety rest in part upon physical competence. Indeed, the increasing acceptance of having a powerful body as a legitimate goal for women is shown in the popularity of jogging and self-defense courses for women. Thus Scott (1974) describes "pride in and control over a finely tuned body" as "the essential source of human self-confidence"; and Mary Duquin (1976) urges that women be helped to "see their bodies as active and able agents to be used to control and direct their destinies." Not only do organized sports increase strength, according to Diana Baumrind (1972), but they provide girls with experiences of teamwork and develop an ability to deal more adequately with success and failure. Similarly, Margaret Hennig (1970), in her study of women executives, found that participation in athletics had been important to all of them in childhood. Women's sports, however, have suffered from a lack of social approval and encouragement and from the absence of proper equipment, training, and facilities. Financial support has been minimal.

A serious consequency of negative social attitudes is the inadequacy of the data about the physical capabilities of women. It is well-established that on the average, males are larger, heavier , and stronger than females. Typically they have less fat, more muscle, denser bone structure, and are able to take in more oxygen to maximize endurance (Scott, 1974)--differences due in large part to the role of androgens. Young girls, however, are at least the equal of boys physically until puberty, when hormonal influences, along with the increasingly sedentary life of many girls, cause boys to begin to surpass them.

In those trained in athletics, however, the gap between males and females is much smaller. In international competitions, sex differences in performance have lessened as women's training has improved. In the Olympic 400 meter freestyle swimming competition, Scott reports, men's time was 16% faster than women's in 1924, but only 7.3% faster in 1972.

Few women are likely to become trained athletes, of course, and the goal for women is certainly not to become as much like male athletes as possible. There is instead a new stress on the benefits of "life sports" for both males and females, that is, sports not requiring large teams and expensive equipment, ones that can be enjoyed over most of a person's life. Opportunities for satisfying participation in athletics can also be broadened by such pragmatic measures as forming age-weight classes in competitions or evaluating broad-jumps by a ratio of distance to body weight (Oglesby, 1976).

Critics of the male model of sports point out that it is intensely competitive and over-institutionalized, stressing what social psychologists call zero-sum games, where one person's gain is another's loss. Sports can be, on the other hand, expressive, playful activities. The ability to play, an important human resource, brings not only learning but a sense of renewal and refreshment. As such, it is characterized by freedom, diversion, the lack of a product, and separateness from real-life consequences--qualities notably lacking in much of contemporary athletics.

The scene is changing. At the time of this writing, a major new scholarly work, *The American Woman in Sport* (Gerber, Felshin, Berlin & Wyrick, 1974), has recently appeared. Moreover, new periodicals on women's sports are appearing --*Sportswoman* and *Women Sports*. Women's magazines are also featuring such articles as "Should Your Daughter Go Out for Football?" (*Family Circle*, October, 1975). One can predict a strengthening of the link between athletics and femininity that will increase women's opportunities in this arena of competence.

Mathematical Competence

No stigma has in the past been attached to the woman who says, "I just can't do mathematics"; indeed, such an attitude has all too often been considered a badge of femininity. Until recently, the serious penalties that ensue have escaped notice. In a survey of the 1973 entering class at Berkeley, Lucy Sells (cited in Ernest, 1976) found that only 8% of women, compared with 57% of men, had had four years of high-school mathematics; thus 92% of the women were barred from 75% of the possible majors. For this reason she called the study of mathematics a "critical filter" for entrance into many desirable careers requiring quantitative skills.

The influences that cause girls to avoid the study of mathematics in the years before college are currently under intensive examination by Lorelei Brush (1977) who has summarized the major factors thought to account for mathematical deficiencies in women: lack of ability; negative attitudes toward mathematics; anxiety; limited career aspirations; stereotypes of mathematicians incompatible with self-images; and low expectation for performance by parents, teachers, and self.

As to ability, investigators who analyze differences in patterns of scores on mathematical aptitude tests find that girls' scores do not begin to fall below those of boys until puberty, and sex differences are greatest in visual-spatial skills. Although the relative genetic and social determinants of this pattern remain unclear,[4] according to Fennema and Sherman (1976) sex differences in innate capacity can in no way account for the magnitude of the discrepancies in the proportions of males and females studying mathematics and entering careers requiring quantitive skills. In a large-scale study of boys and girls in grades 6 to 12, they found no significant sex differences in mathematical achievement. Unlike most previous studies, this one carefully controlled differences in amount of previous training.

With respect to attitudinal influences, John Ernest (1976) found no sex differences in a liking for mathematics up to grade 12. By adolescence, however, girls begin to think of boys as able to do better work in mathematics and to see their fathers rather than their mothers as the "home authority." From then on, mathematics, is increasingly characterized as a male domain. Moreover, girls believe mathematics to be less useful than do boys, and they consider that teachers believe boys can do better work (Fennema & Sherman, 1976). Feeling less confident than boys in their own abilities, they are more likely to attribute their difficulties in mathematics to lack of ability. In spite of all this, girls report as much enjoyment as boys in exercising mathematical competence. Finally, in her studies of anxiety and stereotyping concerning mathematics, Lorelei Brush (1977) has found that, at least at the college level, women are more anxious than men and have self-images more distant from their stereotypes of mathematicians than do men.

The variety of, and uncertainty about, factors contributing to women's problems with mathematics are reflected in the variety of programs aimed at undoing or reversing avoidance of this field (Brush & Baruch, 1977). Among those aimed at college students some have sections "for women only" that provide a supportive and relaxed atmosphere in which students can admit and remedy their puzzlement. One women's college offers a special course for students who had not planned to take college-level mathematics; curriculum materials help students understand the usefulness of mathematic concepts in such diverse fields as music and economics, and they are encouraged to think like creative mathematicians rather than to memorize rules. A mathematics clinic at a co-educational university uses a mental-health model, offering both drop-in and long-term counseling in coordination with special mathematics courses, attempting to reduce negative attitudes and fears while increasing skills. Changes in attitudes are facilitated by "the public acknowledgement that math avoidance is inappropriate in college-educated adults and that math anxiety needs largely to be confronted in order to be cured" (Tobias & Donady, 1977).

Although it is important not to lose this generation of college women to unnecessary "mathophobia," the merits of prevention over cure are obvious. While it appears that negative influences become most acute at puberty, it is clear that efforts must be made at all levels. One must heighten an awareness of the relationship between mathematical skills and access to rewarding careers--equally among parents, teachers, and students--and at the same time one must erase the stereotypes of mathematics as a male domain. Perhaps some day an admission that "I'm no good with figures" will be as embarrassing to adolescent girls as admitting that they can't drive a car.

Implications for Later Life

As to adult women, those who have been reared in traditional fashion often find it difficult to take advantage of new arenas for achievement. An important resource for them is the variety of women's groups that offer a supportive atmosphere where women may discover that others both share their problems and have overcome them. Members typically report improved self-perceptions, increased social skills, a heightened sense of personal worth and effectiveness.[5] In their study of such groups, Lieberman and Bond (1976) found that women joined not because of crises or emergencies in their lives but rather: "to share thoughts and feelings about being a woman," "to learn from other women about their experiences," and "to examine the problems women have with their traditional roles." The opportunity to meet with other women was valued by almost all members, including those who were married, affluent, and successful in their occupations. On this theme, Jessie Bernard (1976) has commented that modern women have been brought up to be oriented toward men early in life and to follow their husbands without protest after marriage, thus creating a void in their attachments to other women. Carroll Smith-Rosenberg (1975) has noted that sex-segregated societies such as that of nineteenth century America are more conducive than our own to the formation of close and supportive relations among women. Thus, the belief among many social scientists that women are incapable of "bonding" ignores the effect of structural forces that facilitate or inhibit such bonds.

Some anthropologists (Tiger, 1969) have argued that bonding is an inherently masculine behavior, arising from the need for men to band together to hunt large animals. In contrast, recent observational studies of several species of non-human primates indicate that females "readily band together against individual males in dominance encounters, thus effectively countering their relative physical powerlessness" (Lancaster, 1976).

The growing tendency of women to draw upon other women as valuable resources in coping with such crises as the birth of a baby, divorce, and widowhood is also evidence against the existence of some innate defect in female bonding capacity. In times of personal change, networks of women act as models, mentors, and simply as friends.

We find it necessary to state explicitly that our messsage is not that competence equals achievement in a male-dominated occupation, nor is it an admonition to get a job and all will be well. We do believe that it is very difficult for anyone restricted solely to the domestic sphere to develop a sense of competence, given the realities of our society. Too many women at various career stages and levels are still struggling to attain a sense of adequacy. Only the ability to take credit for her actual achievements and to meet failure with resistance will enable a woman to meet her needs for the opportunity, respect, and power mentioned early in this book.

Jean Baker Miller (1976) argues that what is most damaging to women is the expectation that they should facilitate the growth of others and serve others at the expense of their own full development. To choose to do so *after* attending to one's growth is quite a different matter. Paradoxically, then, it is just those women who have entered the world outside the home who may be the freest to decide, as they mature, what varieties of commitments they may wish to make.

Notes

[1]There have always been women whose attitudes toward successful achievement are without anxiety and ambivalence. Black women and women with employed mothers have been less likely than other women to be conflicted about achievement or to see inconsistencies between success and femininity or social acceptance (Marshall & Karabenick, 1975). Typically, these women score high in tests of emotional independence--they do not look to or lean on others for their goals.

[2]Early criticisms of Horner's work were directed toward pointing out: the limited forms of success she was studying (academic/professional); the confounding, through use of the medical-school cue, of attitudes toward women who crossed sex-role boundaries into male-dominated fields with attitudes toward success (Tresemer & Pleck, 1972); and the fact that an anagram task performed in an experimental setting could not adequately represent real-life situations (Shaver, 1976). Moreover, since male as well as female subjects were found in a subsequent study to write more fear of success stories when the cue concerned Anne rather than John, it appeared that widely shared attitudes toward women in male-dominated occupations could account for the phenomenon Horner found (Monahan, Kuhn, & Shaver, 1974). Subjects were also found to write fewer fear of success stories when told that half of Anne's class were female, suggesting that deviancy rather than success could be the relevant issue (Lockheed, 1975).

[3]Jacqueline Fleming (in press) reports that, using a newly developed scoring system for the motive to avoid success (Horner, Tresemer, Berens & Watson, 1973), recent studies do find this motive to have a debilitating effect on performance.

[4]Lisa Serbin (1977) points out that providing different toys for boys and girls causes them to experience different levels of practice of certain skills, skills that are relevant for later life. Dolls, for instance, provide fewer opportunities for the practice of spatial relations than do blocks, and spatial relations are important in many occupations.

[5]It is important to note that for some women support groups are inadequate for dealing with the range of issues they may have. Especially helpful to such women have been cognitively oriented therapies which usually consist of several steps. First, either through direct coaching, or, more indirectly, through listening to other women who have similar experiences, they find that problems once thought to be personal can be reconceptualized. Thus, for example, a woman who is employed below her level of skill and is convinced that her work situation reflects a basic lack of drive on her part may come to redefine her plight. She may see that she has underestimated her ability and consequently "stayed put" largely because she focused on her past failures, congruent with her picture of herself as inadequate, and

discounted the successes for which she never took appropriate personal credit. The next step is to realize the pervasiveness of the kind of "attribution" pattern just described. Again a group can facilitate this process. One woman's reconstruction of events in her life can help others recall similar instances. Recall is paired with an awareness of how such an ingrained cognitive set can operate to undermine self-confidence and limit opportunities directly relevant to developing competence.

A more focused therapeutic technique, assertiveness training, grows out of a similar emphasis on learning more direct and effective means of accomplishing personal goals. Here again some unlearning is necessary. People are helped to recognize the long-term negative effects of relying heavily on such interpersonal patterns as accommodation and self-denial, patterns often promoted in the socialization of females. These "underassertive" styles, if utilized extensively, generate resentment, self-doubt, and feelings of worthlessness, and effectively preclude learning that one's own needs are as important as those of others.

Through sharing experiences and role-playing, i.e., practicing new ways of responding to situations where assertiveness would be appropriate, people acquire the social skills and self-perceptions necessary to become more assertive. People who are helped in this way typically report a heightened sense of personal power, feelings of pride, and an increased sense of personal worth.

Afterword

Carolyn G. Heilbrun

Be careful what you wish for in youth, a sage has warned; you may have it in middle age. This homily, delivered as a warning, is also in its way a promise. So, at least, it has been for me. When I was a child in the 1930's and early 1940's, I used to dream of a time when women might share a destiny that did not revolve exclusively around men, might know accomplishment, autonomy, selfhood. Although I was often labelled unconventional, if not blatantly odd, this youthful wish has left me, in middle age, the rich rewards of a professional life. No depreciation of men is here intended. Some of my best friends are men. I have been married to one of the creatures for thirty years, and mother to another for twenty. It is, however, the daughters I am mother to who may now, with more support and sustenance from their generation than I knew, wish for a middle age still alive with the challenges that are, in the end, the breath of life.

But of course, what the inventor of that fine phrase about youth and middle age meant was that we dream simple dreams, and live to experience complex reality. When we are young, we think that success, fame, fortune and beauty are life's prizes. Perhaps they are. But, as Lionel Trilling said, human beings pay in more than equal coin for all they gain or learn in life. This is the human condition. Yet it has been assumed that while the cost of fame, fortune, accomplishment is always worth it for men, it has only rarely been "worth it" for women. This, I think, is a convention women must find the courage to ignore. The Spanish have a proverb: Take what you want, and pay the price. Women have taken little of what are usually considered the bounties of life, apart from marriage and motherhood, because the price has always been proclaimed too high. The price *is* high. But the only impossibly high price may be the one women have in fact always paid: to live a life in which we make nothing happen, but only endure or celebrate what happens *to* us.

The Competent Woman has set forth, as fairly and comprehensively as possible, both what might be taken by women from life, and the price that life may thereupon exact. All the data, so far as I can see, suggest that those women with the greatest sense of fulfillment in life are the ones who did *not* say: I'm going to be a wife and mother when I grow up, but said: I'm going to be--no matter what--a lawyer, truck driver, air-force pilot. Perhaps they did not say it out loud--I know they didn't when I was young--but they wished it, they enacted it, they found themselves. Barnett and Baruch have here collected and ennumerated all the circumstances that seem to lead to that declaration, and all those that prevent the declaration or its carrying out. The authors are honest in their account of the price, more honest than Horatio Alger ever was. What emerges, however, is that though none of the hurdles is easy, the hardest is the first. Most courage is necessary for the decision in adolescence, if not before, to give up a bit of the present for the sake of the future; to ask, not only for the attention of men and boys, but also for the affirmation of one's inner sense of selfhood. Courage is shown too at the moment when the girl determines not to be identified chiefly by her relation to another, as Mrs. John Smith or Johnny's mother, but as herself, Jane Smith, business administrator (it may be). Most men are fathers and sons and husbands, but one does not suggest that their selfhood is identified thereby.

To become a self is no easy matter, but life makes it easier for boys. All circumstances conjoin to push them toward achievement, to a sense of their own singular destiny. Only in the last decade or so have women discovered that, though much of society contrives to keep women inside their kitchens or, if they work outside the home, in poorly paid positions without real possibilities for advancement, there is a force now that will support those women who choose, as they used to say when I was young, to make something of themselves. Perhaps too few of us recognize the importance of the women's movement in this change. Unfortunately, as Eleanor Smeal, President of NOW, recently observed, when the parents of a girl permitted to play Little League ball say, "but we are not for women's lib," or when the professional woman says that she is certainly glad to be a doctor, lawyer, Indian Chief, but she has no time for that feminist nonsense, their denial of those feminists who fought for what these women now have is both unfortunate and sad.

It is amazing, when we stop to consider it, how pervasive are the forces that persuade a woman to pursue domesticity and fulfillment in life through others, how almost secret until very recently have been those forces that whisper that a life of rewarding experience may lie outside the usual "feminine" activities. We have all seen on television--we could scarcely avoid it--the apparent rewards for a shiny kitchen and well-laundered clothes. But only women artists have dared to suggest the pains of unfulfillment. Virginia Woolf, for example, speaks in one novel of how women neither poor nor with young children have time issued to them in "long white ribbons. These they wind round and round and round and round." Emily Dickinson understood the predicament of women without work, with no sense of where they can meaningfully put their lives, sustained perhaps only by volunteer work and tranquilizers:

> *To die--without the Dying*
> *And live--without the Life*
> *That is the hardest miracle*
> *Propounded to Belief*

But these were quiet voices, until lately little heard. The busy years of courtship and early marriage, of young children, of concern mainly with one's appearance and sexuality are, for a time, all absorbing; everything in the media conspires to convince young women that it will be ever thus. Hazlett said that no young man thinks he shall ever die and, it appears, no young woman thinks she shall ever be alone. The danger is a life in which one's ideal of self depends upon the desires of others.

Yet in this book we have, perhaps for the first time, the whole story, both the good news and the bad, about the condition of women in their search for selfhood. The authors assemble for us all that has been statistically and psychologically established, rather than blindly believed. In one of his novels, E.M. Forster speaks of how Beethoven, in his symphonies, always tells us that evil is present in the world, and sometimes conquers. Because Beethoven tells us this, Forster comments, we believe him when he tells us of the joys of life. Thus a book such as this offers truth, which is always less palatable than lies, but in the end more sustaining.

We believe Barnett and Baruch about the rewards of accomplishment, because they have told us about the costs. Having read their survey of all that has been learned about women's competence and achievement, one finishes with the conviction: we must begin here.

Above all, women must learn to build on what has gone before. Perhaps women's greatest problem has been their diffusion. Until fifteen years ago they had not read or heard much of each other's experience, they had not been told that the guilt or discomfort or blighted hope they felt is a universal sentiment, not their own sad secret. Women have not known their own history, nor their own despair, nor built, as men have done, on the experience of one another. It has always seemed to me profoundly significant that as Hecuba speaks in *The Trojan Women* of the pains of womanhood, it is to men she speaks, both on stage and off. The "women" on the stage who hear her, if they do, are about to go off into captivity, and cannot profit from the tragedy.

But where does this leave women in relation to men? Some of us perhaps will choose not to marry: indeed, when Louisa May Alcott was asked what advice she would give to girls, she said she would tell them of the sweet independence of the spinster's life. But for those who will live their life with men as well as women, it is well to notice how often in Barnett and Baruch's study the support and love of men is mentioned: fathers who help their daughters to shape themselves into possibility; mentors who introduce a woman into the old-boy network, husbands who share a woman's life rather than choose to be its object. These men are, as the old phrase goes, "gentle men," and a woman does not discern them by waiting to be wooed or overmastered. True lovers of women are not bullies, a fact too little commented upon. Yet, when all this is noticed, the answer must be with women themselves, who must learn to believe in their dreams, to withstand the assaults of a public world that would rather sell detergents than independence, and a private world whose female inhabitants will hardly proclaim that they themselves have paid too dearly for what they have.

The Competent Woman is badly needed because even those women who are themselves achievers have found it impossible to imagine other women like them. They have assumed that they are freaks, that all other women would rather live in safety, dependent, taken care of; that only they, oddballs, know the joy of risk, the stimulation of competition, the challenge of a world of one's peers. So, for example, when an enormously successful writer like Edna Ferber travelled through the midwest she would imagine the dreams of the farm boy as she passed. Though she herself had dreamed dreams, and worked since she was seventeen, it did not occur to her to imagine a farm girl dreaming. Probably she thought she knew the dreams of women--of popularity, a wedding dress--and did not choose to write of these which she was, as she thought, peculiar enough not to share. It had to be a boy who could be imagined dreaming of individual, perhaps even eccentric, achievement.

All this must change. With the knowledge this book affords, and the wisdom to share with one another our accomplishments and suffering, we may find that women will attain the courage to wish in youth for what in middle age they will still savor with relish: a life, not without risk, but without despair. Women, like men, must confront what Tolkein has told us is the ultimate choice in life. "All we have to decide," he told us, "is what to do with the time that is given us."

Bibliography

Aberle, D.F. & Naegele, F.D. "Middle-class fathers' occupational role and attitudes toward children." *American Journal of Orthopsychiatry,* 1952, *22,* 366-378.

Adams, M. *Single Blessedness.* New York: Basic Books, 1976.

Anderson, J. V. "Psychological determinants." In R. Kundsin (Ed.). *Women and Success.* New York: Morrow, 1974.

Ariès, P. *Centuries of Childhood.* New York: Vantage Books, 1962.

Astin, H. S. *The Woman Doctorate in America.* New York: Russell Sage Foundation, 1969.

Astin, H. S. "Continuing education and the development of adult women." *The Counseling Psychologist,* 1976, *6,* 55-60.

Atkinson, J. W. *An Introduction To Motivation.* Princeton, N.J.: Van Nostrand, 1964.

Atkinson, J. W., & Feather, N. T. *A Theory of Achievement Motivation.* New York: John Wiley, 1966.

Baden, R. K. "No room at the top." *Boston Sunday Globe Magazine,* October 19, 1975.

Bailyn, L. "Career and family orientations of husbands and wives in relation to marital happiness." *Human Relations,* 1970, *23,* 97-113.

Baird, L. *The Graduates.* Princeton, New Jersey: Educational Testing Service, 1973.

Baird, L. "Entrance of women to graduate and professional education." Paper presented at the meeting of the American Psychological Association, Washington, D. C., 1976.

Barnett, R. C. "Sex differences and age trends in occupational preference and occupational prestige." *Journal of Counseling Psychology,* 1975, *22,* 35-38.

Barnett, R. C., & Baruch, G. K. "Empirical literature on occupations and educational aspirations and expectations: A review." Journal Supplement Abstract Service *Catalog of Selected Documents In Psychology,* 1976, *6,* 49.

Barnett, R. C., & Baruch, G. K. "Parental child-rearing values--today and yesterday." Paper presented at the meeting of the Eastern Psychological Association, Washington D.C., 1978

Barnett, R. C., & Baruch, G. K. "Women's work pattern, life satisfaction, and self-esteem: A study of correlates." Paper presented at The Vermont Conference on the Primary Prevention of Psychopathology Burlington, Vermont, 1978.

Baruch, G. K. "Feminine self-esteem, self-ratings of competence, and maternal career-commitment." *Journal of Counseling Psychology,* 1973, *20,* 487-488.

Baruch, G. K. "Maternal influences upon college women's attitudes toward women and work." *Developmental Psychology,* 1972, *6,* 32-37.

Baruch, G. K., "Girls who perceive themselves as competent: Some antecedents and correlates." *Psychology of Women Quarterly,* 1976, *1,* 38-49.

Baruch, G. K., & Barnett, R. C. "Correlates of father involvement in the care of their preschool-age children." Paper presented at the meeting of the Eastern Psychological Association, Washington D.C., 1978.

Baumrind, D. "Patterns of parental authority." *Developmental Psychology Monographs,* 1971, *4,* (1).

Baumrind, D. "From each according to her ability." *School Review,* 1972, *80,* 161-198.

Baumrind, D., & Black, A. E. "Socialization practices associated with dimensions of competence in pre-school boys and girls." *Child Development,* 1967, *38,* 291-327.

Beckman, L. "Values of parenthood among women who want an only child." Paper presented at the meeting of the American Psychological Association, Washington, D. C., 1976.

Bedell, M. "Supermom." *Ms.,* May, 1973.

Beels, C. C. "Whatever happened to father?" *New York Sunday Times,* August 25, 1974.

Bell, S. G. "Expectation of marriage and motherhood: Was it ever enough? A historical study of women in middle age." Paper presented at the West Coast Branch Meeting of the American Historical Association, University of California, La Jolla, 1976.

Bernard, J. *Academic Women.* Cleveland, Ohio: World Publishing Company, 1966.

Bernard, J. *The Future of Marriage.* New York: World-Times, 1972.

Bernard, J. "Homosociality and female depression." Paper presented at the meeting of the American Psychological Association, Washington, D. C., 1976.

Biller, H. B., *Father, Child, and Sex Role.* Lexington, Mass.: D. C. Heath, 1971.

Biller, H. B. *Paternal Deprivation.* Lexington, Mass.: D. C. Heath, 1974.

Biller. H. B., & Meredith, D. *Father Power.* New York: D. McKay, 1974.

Biller, H. B., & Weiss, S. "The father-daughter relationship and the personality development of the female." *Journal of Genetic Psychology,* 1970, *114,* 79-93.

Bird, P. "Images of Women in the Old Testament." In R. R. Ruether (Ed.), *Religion and Sexism.* New York: Simon and Schuster, 1974.

Birnbaum, J. A. "Life patterns and self-esteem in gifted family-oriented and career-committed women." In M. Mednick, S. Tangri, & L. W. Hoffman (Eds.), *Women and Achievement: Social and Motivational Analysis.* New York: Hemisphere-Halsted, 1975.

Block, J. H. "Assessing sex differences: Issues, problems, and pitfalls." *Merrill-Palmer Quarterly,* 1976, *22,* 283-308.

Blood, R. O., Jr., & Wolfe, D. M. *Husbands and Wives.* Glencoe, Ill.: Free Press, 1960.

Bowlby, J. A. *Attachment.* New York: Basic Books, 1969.

Brazelton, T. B. "What makes a good father." *Redbook,* June, 1970.

Brim, O.G.Jr. "Theories of the male mid-life crisis." *The Counseling Psychologist,* 1976, *6,* 2-9.

Bronfenbrenner, U. "Freudian theories of identification and their derivatives." *Child Development,* 1960, *31,* 15-40.

Brophy, J. E., & Goode, T. L. *Teacher-Student Relationships: Causes and Consequences.* New York: Holt, Rinehart, Winston, 1974.

Broverman, I. K., Vogel, S. R., Broverman, D. M., Clarkson, F. E., & Rosenkrantz, P. S. "Sex-role stereotypes: A current appraisal." *Journal of Social Issues,* 1972, *28,* 59-78.

Brown, C. A., Feldberg, R., Fox, E. M., & Kohen, J. "Divorce: Chance of a new lifetime." *Journal of Social Issues,* 1976, *32,* 119-133.

Brown, D. S. "Masculinity-femininity development in children." *Journal of Consulting Psychology,* 1957, *21,* 197-202.

Brown, D. S. "Sex-role development in a changing culture." *Psychological Bulletin,* 1958, *55,* 232-241.

Bruner, J. S. "Nature and uses of immaturity." In K. J. Connolly & J. S. Bruner (Eds.), *The Growth of Competence.* London: Academic Press, 1974.

Brush, L. R. "A path analytic approach to explaining sex differences in students participating in college mathematics." Paper presented at the meeting of the Eastern Psychological Association, Boston, 1977.

Brush, L., & Baruch, G.K. "Encouraging more women to study mathematics." *Radcliffe Quarterly,* June, 1977.

Campbell, A., Converse, P. E., & Rodgers, W. L. *The Quality of American Life.* New York: Russell Sage, 1976.

Carnegie Commission on Higher Education. *Opportunities for Women in Higher Education.* Hightstown, New Jersey: McGraw-Hill, 1973.

Cartwright, L. K. "Conscious factors entering into decisions of women to study medicine." *Journal of Social Issues,* 1972, *28,* 201-215.

Cather, W. *O Pioneers.* Boston: Houghton Mifflin, 1913.

Chevigny, B. G. *The Woman and the Myth: Margaret Fuller's Life and Writings.* New York: The Feminist Press, 1976.

Claudy, J. G. "Cognitive characteristics of the only child." Paper presented at the meeting of the American Psychological Association, Washington, D.C., 1976.

Clifton, M. A., & Smith, H. "Comparison of expressed self-concepts of highly skilled males and females concerning motor performance." *Perceptual and Motor Skills,* 1963, *16,* 199-201.

Collard, E. D. "Achievement motive in the four-year-old child and its relationship to achievement expectancies of the mother." Unpublished doctoral dissertation, University of Michigan, 1964.

Connolly, K. J., & Bruner, J. S., "Competence: Its nature and nurture." In K. J. Connolly & J. S. Bruner (Eds.), *The Growth of Competence*. London: Academic Press, 1974.

Constantini, E., & Craik, K. H. "Women as politicians: The social background, personality, and political careers of female party leaders." *Journal of Social Issues,* 1972, *28,* 217-236.

Coopersmith, S. *The Antecedents of Self-Esteem*. San Francisco: Freeman, 1968.

Cronan, S. "Marriage." In A. Koedt, E. Levine, & A. Rapone (Eds.), *Radical Feminism*. New York: Quadrangle Books, 1973.

Dash, J. *A Life of One's Own*. New York: Harper & Row, 1973.

Davis, L. S., & Spiegler, M. D., "Bright and ambitious: Kiss of death for women?" Paper presented at the meeting of the American Psychological Association, New Orleans, 1974.

Deaux, K., & Emswiller, T. "Explanations of successful performance on sex-linked tasks: What's skill for the male is luck for the female." *Journal of Personality and Social Psychology,* 1974, *29,* 80-85.

Deutsch, H. *The Psychology of Women*. New York: Grune and Stratton, 1944.

Dinitz, S., Dynes, R., & Clarke, A. "Preference for male or female children: Traditional or affectional." *Marriage and Family Living*. 1954, *16,* 128-130.

Dixon, R.B. "Measuring equality between the sexes." *Journal of Social Issues,* 1976, *32,* 19-32.

Dodson, F. *How to Father*. Los Angeles: Nash, 1974.

Drabman, R. S., Hammer, D., & Jarvie, G. J. "Children's perception of media-portrayed sex roles across age." Unpublished manuscript, University of Mississippi, Medical Center.

Duquin, M. E. "Three cultural perceptions of sport." Paper presented at the meeting of the American Psychological Association, Washingon, D. C., 1976.

Dweck, C. S., "Children's interpretation of evaluative feedback: The effects of social cues on learned helplessness." *Merrill-Palmer Quarterly,* 1976, *22,* 105-110.

Epstein, C. F. *Woman's Place*. Berkeley, Calif.: University of California Press, 1971a.

Epstein, C. F. "Women and the professions." In C. F. Epstein & W. J. Goode (Eds.), *The Other Half*. Englewood Cliffs, N. J.: Prentice Hall, 1971b.

Epstein, C. F. "Positive effects of the multiple negative: Explaining the success of black professional women." *American Journal of Sociology,* 1973, *78,* 912-935.

Epstein, C. F. "Bringing women in: Rewards, punishment, and the structure of achievement." In R. Kundsin (Ed.), *Women and Success.* New York: Morrow, 1974.

Ernest, J. "Mathematics and sex." *American Mathematical Monthly,* 1976, *83,* 595-614.

Fagot, B. I., "Teacher reinforcement of feminine-preferred behavior revisited." Paper presented at the meeting of the Society for Research in Child Development, Denver, 1975.

Fagot, B. I., & Patterson, G. B. "An in vivo analysis of reinforcing contingencies for sex-role behaviors in the pre-school child." *Developmental Psychology,* 1969, *1,* 563-568.

Faircloth, C. Cited in *Harvard Law School Bulletin,* February, 1974.

Falbo, T. "Folklore and the only child: A reassessment." Paper presented at the meeting of the American Psychological Association, Washington, D. C., 1976.

Feigen-Fasteau, M. *The Male Machine.* New York: McGraw-Hill, 1974.

Fein, R. "Men's experiences before and after the birth of a first child: Dependence, marital sharing, and anxiety." Unpublished doctoral dissertation, Harvard University, 1973.

Fennema, E., & Sherman, J. "Sex-related differences in mathematics learning: Myths, realities and related factors." In *Women and Mathematics.* Symposium presented at the meeting of the American Association for the Advancement of Science, Boston, 1976.

Feshbach, N. D. "Student teacher preferences for elementary school pupils varying in personality characteristics." *Journal of Educational Psychology,* 1969, *60,* 126-132.

Firestone, S. *The Dialectic of Sex.* New York: Bantam, 1971.

Fleming, J. "Predictive validity of the motive to avoid success in black women." *Humanities,* in press.

Freud, A., & Burlingham, D. *Infants Without Families.* New York: International University Press, 1944.

Frieze, I. H. "Women's expectations for and casual attributions of success and failure." In M. Mednick, S. Tangri, & L. Hoffman (Eds.), *Women and Achievement: Social and Motivational Analysis.* New York: Hemisphere-Halsted, 1975.

Frieze, I. H., McHugh, M., & Duquin, M. "Causal attributions for women and men and sports participation." In E. A. Pepitone (Chair), *Social Psychological Implications of Title IX: Sex Roles and Sports Education.* Symposium presented at the meeting of the American Psychological Association, Washington, D. C., 1976.

Gangsei, D. Personal communication, 1974.

Garai, J. E., & Scheinfeld, A. "Sex differences in mental and behavioral traits." *Genetic Psychology Monographs,* 1968, *77,* 169-299.

Gerber, E. W., Felshin, J., Berlin, P., & Wyrick, W. *The American Woman in Sport.* Reading, Mass.: Addison-Wesley, 1974.

Glick, P. C., "A demographer looks at American families." *Journal of Marriage and the Family,* 1975, *37,* 15-26.

Goodenough, E. W. "Interest in persons as an aspect of sex differences in the early years." *Genetic Psychology Monographs,* 1957, *55,* 287-323.

Graham, P. A. "Women in academe." *Science,* 1970, *169,* 1284-1290.

Graham, P. A. "So much to do: Guides for historical research on women in higher education." *Teachers College Record,* 1975, *76,* 422-429.

Greenberg, M., & Norris, N. "Engrossment: The newborn's impact upon the father." *American Journal of Orthopsychiatry,* 1974, *44,* 520-531.

Gross, N., & Trask, A. E. *The Sex Factor and the Management of Schools.* New York: John Wiley, 1976.

Gutmann, D. "Men, women and the parental imperative." *Commentary,* 1973, *56,* 59-64.

Guttentag, M., & Bray, H. *Undoing Sex Stereotypes.* New York: McGraw-Hill, 1976.

Harris, P. R. "Problems and solutions in achieving equality for women." In W. T. Furniss & P. A. Graham (Eds.), *Women in Higher Education.* Washington D. C.: American Council on Education, 1974.

Harris, T. G. "A conversation with Margaret Mead." *Psychology Today,* July, 1970.

Harrison, B. "Feminist experiments in education." In J. Stacey, S. Bereaud, & J. Daniels (Eds.), *And Jill Came Tumbling After: Sexism in American Education.* New York: Dell, 1974.

Hart, M. "Sport: Women sit in the back of the bus." *Psychology Today,* October, 1971.

Hartley, R. E., & Klein, A. "Sex-role concepts among elementary school-age girls." *Marriage and Family Living,* 1959, *21,* 59-64.

Helson, R. "Women mathematicians and the creative personality." *Journal of Consulting and Clinical Psychology,* 1971, *36,* 210-220.

Helson, R. "The changing image of the career woman." *Journal of Social Issues,* 1972, *28,* 33-46.

Hennig, M. "Career development for women executives." Unpublished doctoral dissertation, Graduate School of Business Administration, Harvard University, 1970.

Hennig, M. "Family dynamics and the successful woman executive." In R. Kundsin (Ed.), *Women and Success.* New York: Morrow, 1974.

Hennig, M., & Jardim A. *The Managerial Woman.* New York: Anchor/Doubleday, 1977.

Herzog, E., & Sudia, C. "Children in fatherless families." In B. M. Caldwell & H. N. Ricciuti (Eds.), *Review of Child Development Research* (Vol. 3), Chicago: University of Chicago, 1974.

Hetherington, E. M. "Effects of father absence on personality development in adolescent daughters." *Developmental Psychology,* 1972, *7,* 313-326.

Hetherington, E. M., Cox, M., & Cox, R. "The aftermath of divorce." Paper presented at the meeting of the American Psychological Association, Washingtion, D. C., 1976.

Hochschild, A. "Making it: Marginality and obstacles to minority consciousness." In R. Kundsin (Ed.), *Women and Success.* New York: Morrow, 1974.

Hoffman, L. W. "Effects of the employment of mothers on parental power relations and the division of household tasks." *Journal of Marriage and Family Living,* 1960, *22,* 27-35.

Hoffman, L. W. "Early childhood experiences and women's achievement motives." *Journal of Social Issues,* 1972, *28,* 129-156.

Hoffman, L. W. "The professional woman as mother." In R. Kundsin (Ed.), *Women and Success.* New York: Morrow, 1974a.

Hoffman, L. W. "The effects of maternal employment on the child: A review of the research." *Developmental Psychology,* 1974b, *10,* 204-228.

Hoffman, L. W. "Fear of success in males and females: 1965 and 1971." *Journal of Consulting and Clinical Psychology,* 1974c, *42,* 353-358.

Hoffman, L. W. "Changes in family roles, socialization, and sex differences." *American Psychologist,* 1977, *32,* 644-657.

Holstrom, L. L. *The Two-Career Family.* Cambridge, Mass.: Schenkman, 1972.

Horner, M. "Sex differences in achievement and performance in competitive and noncompetitive situations." Unpublished doctoral dissertation, University of Michigan, 1968.

Horner, M. S. "Toward an understanding of achievement related conflicts in women." *Journal of Social Issues,* 1972, *28,* 157-175.

Horner, M. S., Tresemer, D. W., Berens, A. E. & Watson, R. "Scoring manual for an empirically derived scoring system for motive to avoid success." Unpublished manuscript, Harvard University, 1973.

Joffee, C. "As the twig is bent." In J. Stacey, S. Bereaud, & J. Daniels (Eds.), *And Jill Came Tumbling After: Sexism in American Education,* New York: Dell, 1974.

Johnson, M. "Sex-role learning in the nuclear family." *Child Development,* 1963, *34,* 319-333.

Kagan, J. "The concept of identification." *Psychological Review,* 1958, *65,* 296-305.

Kagan, J., Kearsley, R., & Zelazo, P. "The effects of infant day care on psychological development." Paper presented at the meeting of the American Association for the Advancement of Science, Boston, 1976.

Kagan, J., & Lemkin, J. "The child's differential perception of parental attributes." *Journal of Abnormal and Social Psychology,* 1960, *61,* 440-447.

Kagan, J., & Moss, H. A. *Birth to Maturity.* New York: John Wiley, 1962.

Kangas, J., & Bradway, K. "Intelligence at middle age: A thirty-eight-year follow-up." *Developmental Psychology,* 1972, *5,* 333-337.

Kanter, R. M. *Men and Women of the Corporation.* New York: Basic Books, 1977.

Keith-Spiegel, P., Fidell, L. S., & Hoffman, D. "Choosing the sex of offspring: Possible implications for feminist goals." Paper presented at the meeting of the American Psychological Association, New Orleans, August, 1974.

Kohlberg, L. "A cognitive-developmental analysis of children's sex-role concepts and attitudes," In E. Macobby (Ed.), *The Development of Sex Differences.* Stanford, Calif.: Stanford University Press. 1966.

Kohlberg, L., & Ullian, D. Z. "Stages in the development of psychosexual concepts and attitudes." In R. C. Friedman, R. M. Richant, & R. L. Vande Wiele (Eds.), *Sex Differences in Behavior.* New York: John Wiley, 1974.

Komarovsky, M. *Blue Collar Marriage.* New York: Random House, 1962.

Kotelchuck, M. "The nature of the child's tie to his father." Unpublished doctoral dissertation, Harvard University, 1972.

Kotin, A. "Divorce: Eternal busyness." *Radcliffe Quarterly,* June, 1976.

Kundsin, R. (Ed.), *Women and Success.* New York: Morrow, 1974.

Lamb, M. E. "The one-year-old's interaction with its parents." Paper presented at the meeting of the Eastern Psychological Association, New York, 1976a.

Lamb, M. E. *The Role of the Father in Child Development.* New York: John Wiley, 1976b.

Lancaster, J. B. "Sex roles in primate societies." In M. S. Teitelbaum (Ed.), *Sex Differences: Social and Biological Perspectives.* New York: Anchor, 1976.

Lein, L. Personal Communication, 1977.

Leonard, M. "Fathers and daughters." *International Journal of Psychoanalysis,* 1966, *47,* 325-334.

Lester, M., Kotelchuck, M., Spelke, E., Sellers, M. J., & Klein, R. E. "Separation protest in Guatemalan infants: Cross-cultural and cognitive findings." *Developmental Psychology,* 1974, *10.* 79-85.

Lever, J. "Sex differences in the games children play." *Social Problems,* 1976, *23,* 478-487.

Levine, J. L. *Who will Raise the Children? New Options for Fathers (and mothers).* Philadelphia: J. P. Lippincott Co., 1976.

Lewis, E. *Developing Woman's Potential.* Ames, Iowa: Iowa State University Press, 1968.

Lewis, M., Weinraub, M., & Ban, P. *Mothers and Fathers, Girls and Boys: Attachment Behavior in the First Two Years of Life.* Princeton, N.J.: Educational Testing Service, 1972.

Levitin, T. E., & Chananie, J. D., "White middle-class suburban teacher-liking." *Child Development,* 1972, *43,* 1309-1316.

Lieberman, M. A., & Bond, A. R. "The problem of being a woman: A survey of 1,700 women in consciousness-raising groups." *Journal of Applied Behavioral Science,* 1976, *12,* 363-379.

Lightfoot, S. L. "Sociology of education: Perspectives on women." In M. Millman & R. M. Kanter (Eds.), *Another Voice.* Garden City, N.Y.: Anchor Press, 1975.

Lightfoot, S. L. "Socialization and education of young black girls in school." *Teachers College Record,* 1976, *78,* 239-262

Lipman-Blumen, J. "The development and impact of female role ideology." Paper presented at the Radcliffe Institute Conference: *Women: Resource for a Changing World.* Cambridge, Mass., 1972.

Lipman-Blumen, J. "Toward a homosocial theory of sex roles: An explanation of the sex segregation of social institutions." *Signs,* 1976, *1,* 15-32.

Lloyd, C. B. "Women's work." *Bryn Mawr Alumnae Bulletin,* Winter, 1975, 2-7.

Lloyd, S. *Abbot Academy: The Biography of a School, 1829-1973.* In press.

Lockheed, M. E. "Female motive to avoid success: A psychological barrier or a response to deviancy?" *Sex Roles,* 1975, *1,* 41-50.

Lynn, D. B. *The Father: His Role in Child Development.* Belmont, Calif.: Brooks/Cole, 1974.

Maccoby, E. E., & Jacklin, C. N. *The Psychology of Sex Differences.* Stanford, Calif.: Stanford University Press, 1974.

Marshall, J. M., & Karabenick, S. A. "Self-esteem, fear of success, and occupational choice in female adolescents." Unpublished manuscript, Eastern Michigan University, 1975.

McClelland, D. C. *Power: The Inner Experience.* New York: Irvington, 1975.

McClelland, D. C., Atkinson, J. W., Clark, R. A., & Lowell, E. L. *The Achievement Motive.* New York: Irvington, 1976.

McDonagh, E. "Patterns of achievement of nineteenth-century American women." Paper presented at Radcliffe Institute Colloquium, Cambridge, Mass.: 1975.

Morgan, S.W., & Mauser, B. "Behavioral and fantasized indicators of avoidance of success in men and women." Paper presented at the meeting of the Eastern Psychological Association, Boston, 1972.

Miller, J. B. *Toward a New Psychology of Women.* Boston: Beacon Press, 1976.

Moss, H. A. "Sex, age, and state as determinants of mother-infant interaction." *Merrill-Palmer Quarterly,* 1967, *13,* 19-36.

Murphy-Berman, V. "Effects of success and failure on perceptions of gender identity." *Sex Roles,* 1976, *2,* 367-374.

Nadelson, T., & Eisenberg, L. "The successful professional woman: On being married to one." *American Journal of Psychiatry,* 1977, *134,* 1071-1076.

Nash, J. "The father in contemporary culture and current psychological literature." *Child Development,* 1965, *56,* 261-297.

Ngai, S. Y. "Long distance commuting as a solution to geographical limitation to career choices of two-career families." Unpublished master's thesis, Massachusetts Institute of Technology, 1974.

Nochlin, L. "Why are there no great women artists?" In V. Gornick & B. K. Moran (Eds.), *Woman in Sexist Society.* New York: Basic Books, 1971.

Nye, F. I. "Sociocultural context." In L. W. Hoffman & F. I. Nye (Eds.), *Working Mothers.* San Francisco; Jossey-Bass, 1974.

Nye, F. I., & Hoffman, L. W. (Eds.), *The Employed Mother in America.* Chicago: Rand McNally, 1963.

Oglesby, C. A. "Jocks and jockarinas: Will you really need a program to tell the difference?" Paper presented at the meeting of the American Psychological Association, Washington, D. C., 1976.

O'Leary, V. E. "Some attitudinal barriers to occupational aspirations in women." *Psychological Bulletin,* 1974, *81,* 809-826.

Osofsky, J. D., & O'Connell, E. J. "Parent child interaction: Daughters' effects upon mothers' and fathers' behaviors." *Developmental Psychology,* 1972, *7,* 157-168.

Papanek, H. "The two person career." *American Journal of Sociology,* 1973, *78,* 852-872.

Parsons, J. E., Ruble, D. N., Hodges, K. L., & Small, A. W. "Cognitive-developmental factors in emerging sex differences in achievement-related expectancies." *Journal of Social Issues,* 1976, *32,* 47-61.

Parsons, T. "Family structure and the socialization of the child." In T. Parsons & R. F. Bales (Eds.), *Family, Socialization and Interaction Process.* Glencoe, Ill.: Free Press, 1955.

Pedersen, F. A., "Beyond father absence: Conceptualizations of father effects." Paper presented at the meeting of the Society for Research in Child Development, Denver, 1975.

Pedersen, F. A., & Robson, K. "Father participation in infancy." *American Journal of Orthopsychiatry,* 1969, *39,* 466-472.

Peer Perspective, November, 1976.

Peplau, L. A. "The impact of fear of success, sex-role attitudes and opposite sex relationships on women's intellectual performance: An experimental study of competition in dating couples." Unpublished doctoral dissertation, Harvard University, 1973.

Pleck, J. H., & Sawyer, J. *Men and Masculinity.* Englewood Cliffs, N.J.: Prentice-Hall, 1974

Poor, R. (Ed.), *Four Days, Forty Hours; Reporting a Revolution in Work and Leisure.* Cambridge, Mass.: Bursk & Poor, 1970.

Rapoport, R., & Rapoport, R. *Dual-Career Families.* Baltimore: Penguin,1971.

Ravitch, D. "The public school's tasks and how they grew." *New York Times,* Sunday, November 17, 1975.

Reed, A. Cited in *Harvard Law School Bulletin*, February, 1974.

Reed, J. "Margaret Sanger." Paper presented at the Second Berkshire Conference on the History of Women, Cambridge, Mass. 1974.

Rich, A. *Of Woman Born.* New York: W. W. Norton, 1976.

Ricks, F. A., & Pyke, S. W. "Teacher perceptions and attitudes that foster or maintain sex role differences." *Interchange,* 1973, 4, 26-33.

Rodzinski, H. Our Two Lives. New York: Scribner, 1976.

Romer, N. "The motive to avoid success and its effects on performance in school-age males and females." *Developmental Psychology,* 1975, *11,* 689-699.

Rosaldo, M. Z., & Lamphere, L. *Woman, Culture, and Society.* Palo Alto, Calif.: Stanford University Press, 1974.

Rosen, B. C. "The achievement syndrome: A psychocultural dimension of social stratification." *American Sociological Review,* 1956, *21,* 203-211.

Rosenberg, M. *Society and the Adolescent Self-Image.* Princeton, N. J.: Princeton University Press, 1965.

Rossi, A. S. "Barriers to the career choice of engineering, medicine, or science among American women." In J. A. Mattfeld & C. G. Van Aken (Eds.), *Women in the Scientific Professions.* Cambridge, Mass.: MIT Press, 1965.

Rubin, J. Z., Provenzano, F., & Luria, Z. "The eye of the beholder: Parents' views on sex of newborns." *American Journal of Orthopsychiatry,* 1974, *44,* 512-519.

Sarrio, T. N., Jacklin C. N., & Tittle C. K. "Sex role stereotyping in the public schools." *Harvard Educational Review.* 1973, *43*, 386-416.

Safilios-Rothchild, C. "The influence of the wife's degree of work commitment upon some aspects of family organization and dynamics." *Journal of Marriage and the Family,* 1970, *32*, 681-691.

Schmuck, P. A. "Deterrents to women's careers in school management." *Sex Roles*, 1975, *1,* 339-354.

Schneider, L. "Our failures only marry." In J. Stacey, S. Bereaud, & J. Daniels (Eds.) *And Jill Came Tumbling After: Sexism in American Education.* New York: Dell, 1974.

Scott, A. C. "Closing the muscle gap." *Ms.*, March, 1974.

Sears, P. S., & Barbee, A. H. "Career and life satisfaction among Terman's gifted women." In J. Stanley, W. George, & C. Solano (Eds.) *The Gifted and the Creative: Fifty-Year Perspective.* Baltimore, Md.: Johns Hopkins University Press, 1977.

Serbin, L. A. "Sex role socialization and psychopathology." Paper presented at the meeting of the American Psychological Association, New Orleans, 1974.

Serbin, L. "Sex stereotyped play behavior in the pre-school classroom." Paper presented at the meeting of the Society for Research in Child Development, New Orleans, 1977.

Sexton, P. C. *The Feminized Male.* New York: Random House, 1969.

Sherman, J. "Girls' attitudes toward mathematics: Implications for counseling." Paper presented at the meeting of the American Psychological Association, Washington, D. C., 1976.

Shaver, P. "Questions concerning fear of success and its conceptual relatives." *Sex Roles,* 1976, *2,* 305-320.

Sklar, K. K. "The founding of Mt. Holyoke female seminary: A study in the history of female education in New England, 1790-1837." Paper presented at Mt. Holyoke College and South Hadley, Massachusetts Bicentennial Celebration, 1976.

Smith, J. "Dates with 'guinea pigs.'" *San Francisco Chronicle,* April 26, 1971.

Smith, M. B., "Competence and socialization." In J. A. Clausen (Ed.), *Socialization and Society.* Boston: Little, Brown, 1968.

Smith-Rosenberg, C. "The female world of love and ritual: Relations between women in 19th century America." *Signs,* 1975, *1,* 1-30.

Smith-Rosenberg, C., & Rosenberg, C. "The female animal." *Journal of American History,* 1973, *2,* 332-356.

Spence, J. T., & Helmreich, R. "Who likes competent women? Competence, sex-role congruence of interests and subjects' attitudes toward women as determinants of interpersonal attraction." *Journal of Applied Social Psychology,* 1972, *2,* 197-213.

Spitz, R. A. "Hospitalism: An inquiry into the genesis of psychiatric conditions in early childhood. *Psychoanalytic Study of the Child,* 1945, *1,* 53-74.

Spock, B. M. *The Common Sense Book of Baby and Child Care.* New York: Duell, Sloan, & Pearce, 1946.

Sprung, B. *Guide to Non-Sexist Early Childhood Education.* New York: The Women's Action Alliance, 1974.

Staines, G., Tavris, C., & Jayaratne, T. "The queen bee syndrome." *Psychology Today,* 1974.

Stein, A. H., & Bailey, M. M. "The socialization of achievement orientation in females." *Psychological Bulletin,* 1973, *80,* 345-366.

Stein, B., Cohen, A., & Gadon, H. "Flextime: Work when you wish." *Psychology Today,* June, 1976.

Steinmann, A., & Fox, D. "Male-female perceptions of the female role in the United States." *Journal of Psychology,* 1966, *64,* 265-276.

Sternglanz, S. H., & Lyberger-Ficek, S. "Sex differences in student-teacher interactions in the college classroom." *Sex Roles,* 1977, *3,* 345-352.

Tasch, R. J. "The role of the father in the family." *Journal of Experimental Education,* 1952, *20,* 319-361.

Taylor, S., & Fiske, S. T. "The token in a small group: Research findings and theoretical implications." In J. Sweeney (Ed.), *Psychology and Politics.* New Haven: Yale, 1976.

Thomas, A. H., & Stewart, N. R. "Counselor response to female clients with deviate and conforming career goals." *Journal of Counseling Psychology,* 1971, *18,* 352-357.

Thomas, M. C. "Present tendencies in women's college and university education." In J. Stacey, S. Bereaud, & J. Daniels (Eds.), *And Jill Came Tumbling After: Sexism in American Education.* New York: Dell, 1974.

Thompson, C. "The role of women in our culture." In P. Mullahy (Ed.), *A Study of Interpersonal Relations.* New York: Hermitage, 1949.

Thorndike, E. L. *Notes on Child Study.* New York: Macmillan, 1903.

Tidball, M. E. "Perspective on academic women and affirmative action." *Educational Record,* 1973, *54,* 130-135.

Tiger, L. *Men in Sports.* London: Nelson, 1969.

Tittle, C. K. "Sex bias in educational measurement: Fact or fiction." *Measurement and Evaluation in Guidance,* 1974, *6,* 219-226.

Tobias, S., & Donady, B. "Counselling the math anxious." Unpublished manuscript, Wesleyan University, 1977.

Tresemer, D. "The cumulative record of research on 'fear of success'." *Sex Roles,* 1976, *2,* 217-236.

Tresemer, D., & Pleck, J. "Maintaining and changing sex-role boundaries in men (and women)." Paper presented at the Radcliffe Institute Conference: *Women: Resource for a Changing World.* Cambridge, Mass., 1972.

Trivers, R. L. "Parental investment and sexual selection." In B. Campbell (Ed.), *Sexual Selection and the Descent of Man.* Chicago: Aldine, 1972.

Turner, B. G. "Socialization and career orientation among black and white college women." Paper presented at the meeting of the American Psychological Association, Honolulu, Hawaii, 1972.

Tyack, D. *The One Best System.* Cambridge: Harvard University Press, 1974.

Tyack, D. "Some approaches to the history of the education of women." Unpublished paper, Stanford University, 1975.

Vaughter, R., Gubernick, D., Matossian, J., & Haslett, B. "Sex differences in academic expectations and achievement." Paper presented at the meeting of the American Psychological Association, New Orleans, 1974.

Veroff, J., & Feld, S. *Marriage and Work In America.* New York: Van Nostrand Reinhold, 1970.

Vogel, S. R., Broverman, I., Broverman, D., Clarkson, F., & Rosenkrantz, P. "Maternal employment and perceptions of sex-role stereotypes." *Developmental Psychology,* 1970, *3,* 384-391.

Wallston, B. "The effects of maternal employment on children." *Journal of Child Psychology and Psychiatry,* 1973, *14,* 81-95 .

Walsh, M. R. *"Doctors Wanted: No Women Need Apply": Sexual Barriers in the Medical Profession, 1835-1975.* New Haven: Yale, 1977.

Weiner, B., Frieze, I., Kukla, A., Reed, L., Rest, S., & Rosenbaum, R. *Perceiving the Causes of Success and Failure.* New York: General Learning, 1971.

Weingarten, K. "Similarly and dissimilarly employed couples: Interaction patterns in two-career couples." Unpublished doctoral dissertation, Harvard University, 1975.

Westoff, C. F., Potter, R. G., & Sagi, P. C. *The Third Child: A Study in the Prediction of Fertility.* Princeton: Princeton University Press, 1963.

Westoff, C. F., & Rindfuss, R. R. "Sex preselection in the United States: Some implications." *Science,* 1974, *184,* 633-636.

White, R. W. "Motivation reconsidered: The concept of competence." *Psychological Review,* 1959, *66,* 297-333.

Whiting, B. B. "Changing life styles in Kenya." *Daedelus,* 1977, *106,* 211-225.

Whiting, J. W. M. "Resource mediation and learning by identification." In I. Iscoe & H. Stevenson (Eds.), *Personality Development in Children.* Austin, Texas: University of Texas Press, 1960.

Whiting, J. W. Personal communication, 1975.

Winchell, R., Fenner, D., & Shaver, P. "Impact of coeducation on 'fear of success' imagery expressed by male and female high school students." *Journal of Educational Psychology,* 1974, *66,* 726-730.

Wylie, P. C. "Children's estimates of their schoolwork ability as a function of sex, race, and socioeconomic level." *Journal of Personality,* 1963, *31,* 203-224.

Index

Aberle, D. F., 62
achievement
    approval and, 42
    barriers to, 136
    co-education and, 120, 124
    motivation, 99, 131, 134-135
    vicariousness in, 94-95
Adams, M., *Single Blessedness,* 99
adolescence
    family relationships during, 65, 83-84
    stereotyping in, 129
    at marriage, 76, 82, 88, 89
    sex role restrictions and, 68n5
    see also life cycle
aggression
    of fathers, 56
    in women, 21, 37
Alcott, L. M., 156
Alger, H., 153
American Woman in Sport, The
    (Gerber, Felshin, Berlin and
    Wyrick), 145
Anderson, J. V., 34
anthropology, mother role and, 70-74
anxiety, 64, 136, 147
Ariès, P., 89
Aristotle, 143
    Physiognomics, 142
assertiveness
    child-rearing and, 85-86
    as masculine attribute, 19-20, 74
    of women, 97, 142
Astin, H., 26, 37, 130

athletes and athletics, 5
    fathers and, 55
    girls discouraged from, 24, 131
    women and, 45, 143-145
    see also games; play and playfulness
Atkinson, J. W., 134, 140
attitude(s)
    behavior and, 17
    changes in, 76-77
    as constraint, 37-38, 133
    labor supply and, 15
    parental, 59-60, 62-63, 80-81
    sex differences in, 17-18
    toward success, 140, 150n1
    toward women's education, 109,
        110-111
    of women toward women, 45-46
attribution patterns, 132-133, 141-142
authority
    women and, 18-19, 44-45
    by women over men, 37-38
autonomy
    child-rearing and, 80-81, 83-84, 85-86
    divorce and, 100-101
    singleness and, 98-99

Baden, R. K., 113, 116-117
Bailey, M. M., 135
Bailyn, L., 98
Ballard, E. D., 31
Ban, P., 65, 80
Barbee, A. H., 100
Barnett, R. C., 62, 66, 80, 82, 132, 133

Baruch, G. K., 17, 62, 66, 80, 82, 85, 104, 132, 147
Baumrind, D., 85, 143
Beckman, L., 102
Bedell, M., 43
Beels, C. C., 54
behavior(s)
    dependent, 74, 79-80, 81-82, 83-84
    education and, 121, 124-125
    toward female children, 62
    sex differences in, 17-18, 65
Bell, S. G., 30, 31, 33, 43, 50n1
Berlin, P., *American Woman in Sport, The,* 145
Berman, A., 38
Bernard, J., 39, 86, 98,99, 126, 148
Bible, 60, 63
Biller, H. B., 52, 54
    Father Power, 67n1
biologists, on father role, 56
Bird, P., 60
Birnbaum, J. A., 40, 49, 74, 97, 99
birth order
    IQ and, 103
    as success factor, 28
birth rate, 76, 89, 102
birth ratio, 79
Black, E. A., 85
black women
    success and, 29, 150n1
    women's movement and, vi
Block, J. H., 87n1
Blood, R. O., 96
Bond, A. R., 148
bonding, among women, 148-149
Bonheur, R., 32, 45
Boston Globe, 38, 39, 40, 41, 78, 89
Boston School Committee, 114
Bowlby, J., 75
boys, *see* sons
Bradway, K., 16
Bray, H., 128
Brazleton, T. B., 55-56
Brim, O., 18
bris, *see* circumcision
Bronfenbrenner, U., 82
Brophy, J. E., 125
Broverman, D. M., 19, 104
Boverman, I. K., 19, 104
Brown, C. A., "Divorce: Chance of a New Lifetime," 101
Brown, D., 66, 77
Bruner, J., 14
Brush, L., 146, 147
Bryn Mawr College, 109, 115

Campbell, A., 96, 102
Carnegie Commission, 113
Cartwright, L. K., 26, 34
Cather, W., *O Pioneers,* 27
Chananie, J. D., 124
Chevigny, B. G., 32
Child-care
    father role in, 54, 56, 66-67, 94
    in hunter-gatherer societies, 72
    tax deductibility for, 36-37
    see also child-rearing; day care
        centers; *entries under family roles*
child development theory, father role
    and, 58
child-rearing
    of competent daughters, 85-86
    divorce and, 100-102
    father role in, 104
    female dependence encouraged in,
        28, 29, 30, 79-80
    in hunter-gatherer societies, 72
    sex differences in, 65, 78-79, 80-84
    successful women and, 43
    value of, 15, 20
    see also child-care; *entries under
        family roles*
children
    economic value of, 71, 72, 73
    of one-child family, 102-103
    vicariousness and, 94-95
    see also daughters; sons
circumcision (*bris*), 61, 62
Clark, R. A., 134
Clarke, A., 59
Clarkson, F. E., 19, 104
class
    female success related to, 26, 27
    marriage and, 99, 105n2, 105n6
    sex as basis for, 93
    see also middle-class(es); working-
        class(es)
Claudy, J. G., 103
Clifton, M. A., 17
clothing, women and, 45
cognition and perception
    children's, of parents, 66-67, 82-83
    work situations and, 44-45
cognitive deprivation, 15-16
Cohen, A., 47
Collard, E. D., 80
colleges and universities
    career opportunities in, 34-36
    maternity leave and, 47-48
    for women, 115, 120, 121, 147
    women's oppression and, 108, 114
"commuting couples," 97, 105n4

competition
    athletics and, 145
    in children's games, 24-25, 131
    discouragement of, 21
    division of labor and, 92, 95-96
    mixed-sex, 137
    mother/daughter, 65, 83-84
    of only children, 103
    among women, 46
congresswomen, 36, 38, 40
Connolly, K., 14
Constantini, E., 26
Converse, P. E., 96
Coopersmith, S., 17, 85
Craik, K. H., 26
Cronan, S., 93
curricula
    mathematics and, 147
    sexism in, 111, 122, 127

D'Andrade, 50n6
Dash, J., 32
daughters
    fathers and, 52-53, 66-67, 81, 82-83
    mothers and, 79-81, 82-83
    preference for, 61-62
    psychological characteristics of,
        79-80
    role of, in traditional family, 54, 82
    sexuality of, 63-65
    of working mothers, 103-104
Davis, L. S., 139
day-care centers, 104-105, 106n10, 127
    see also child care
Deaux, K., 141
dependence, 18-19
    in classroom, 124, 125
    in mother/daughter relationship,
        79-81, 83-84
    in mother role, 74
depression, in women, 15-16
deprivation, achievement and, 134
Deutsch, H., 110
Dickinson, E., 155
Dinitz, S., 59, 77
discrimination
    Civil Service and, 41
    Education Amendment Act and, 143
    nepotism regulations and, 36
    Smith College and, 115
divorce
    effect of, on daughters, 53
    labor market and, 100-101
    problems of, 100-102, 105n3
    rates of, 88, 89
    remarriage and, 100

"Divorce: Chance of a New Lifetime"
    (Brown, Feldberg, Fox and
    Kohen), 101
Dixon, R. B., 91
Dodson, F., How to Father, 55
Donady, B., 147
Drabman, R. S., 129
"dual-career couples," 97-98, 105n3
Duquin, M., 143
Dweck, C., 141
Dynes, R., 59

education
    attributes and, 141-142
    co-educational, 119-121
    competency and, 112-113
    divorce and, 100-101
    exclusion of women from, 34-35,
        78-79, 108-110, 111-112
    history of, in U.S., 107-110, 114-115
    increase of women receiving, 76, 89
    of middle-class women, 94-95
    parental expectations and, 62-63
    singleness and, 100
educational system
    proportion of women in, 113, 120
    school boards of, 118
    sexism in, 113-116
education (elementary)
    administration of, 113
    restricted for women, 108
    sexism in, 122, 127
    teachers in, 125
education (secondary)
    girls in, 83, 110
    teachers in, 125-126
efficiency, as masculine trait, 74
egalitarianism, 21
    in family relationship, 61, 98
    school system and, 107, 111
ego (male), psychological superiority
    and, 40-41
Eisenberg, L., 105n5
elementary education, see education
    (elementary)
Emswiller, T., 141
Engels, F., 93
engineers, per cent of women as, 23
engrossment, phenomenon of, 56-57
envy, dual-career couples and, 97, see
    also penis envy; rivalry
Epstein, C. G., 29, 42, 45, 91
Equal Rights Amendment, 38
Ernest, J., 145, 146
exclusion, see isolation
executives (women), 45-46

backgrounds of, 26-27, 32-33, 144
family life of, 33-34, 83-84
protege system and, 39-40
"expectancy-value theory," 135
expectation, success and, 141
experience, sex differences in, 25

Fagot, B. I., 124
failure, attribution of, 140
Faircloth, C., 39
Falbo, T., 103
family
    child-centered, 75
    childless, 102, 106n8, 106n9
    feminine leadership and, 19
    feminist view of, 93-94
    genetic view of roles in, 90-91
    satisfactions of, 96-98
    sharing of power in, 96
    of successful women, 33-34
sociological theory and, 92
traditional, 82, 88-89
    see also entries under individual
        family roles
Family Circle magazine, 64, 145
family size, 68n2, 89, 102, 106n9
family structure
    female success related to, 26, 28-29
    shifts in patterns of, 88-89
Father Power (Biller and Meredith),
    67n1
fathers
    absence of, 52-53, 54, 56, 105n7
    birth of females and, 59-60
    child-care role of, 54, 56, 57-59, 62,
        104
    daughters and, 52-53, 66-67, 80-81,
        82-83
    male child preference and, 59-60,
        61-62
    sex role definition and, 82-83
    sexuality and, 63-65
    of successful women, 30-33, 50n5
Feather, N. T., 135
Feigen-Fasteau, M., 65
    Male Machine, The, 67n1
Fein, Robert, 59, 61
Feld, S., 105n2
Feldberg, R., "Divorce: Chance of a
    New Lifetime," 101
Felshin, J., American Woman in
    Sport, The, 145
femininity
    attributes of, 19-20, 44, 74, 78-79
    education and, 110, 120-121, 123,
        124

in female child, 63, 79, 80-81
    mathematics and, 145-146
    mother/daughter relationship and,
        83-84
    power (authority) and, vii, 19, 44-45
    success and, 32-33, 37-38, 40-41, 136
feminists and feminism, vii, 45, 50n4,
    127, 143
    stereotypes and, 122
    view of marriage among, 93-94
Feminized Male, The (Sexton), 112
Fennema, E., 146
Fenner, D., 121
Fenwick, M., 38
Ferber, E., 157
fertility rate, see birth rate
Feshbach, N. D., 124
Fidell, L. S., 50n4
Firestone, S., 93
Fiske, S. T., 44
Fleming, J., 150n3
Foote, A., 72-73
foreign parentage, 26-28
Forster, E. M., 155
foster care, 75-76
four-day week, 47
Fox, E. M., "Divorce: Chance of New
    Lifetime," 101
fragility, stereotype of, 79
Freud, A., 75
Frieze, I., 140, 141, 143
fringe benefits, 47-48
Fuller, M., 32

Gaden, H., 47
games, sex difference in, 24, 127
    see also athletes and athletics; play
        and playfulness
Gangsei, D., 61
Garai, J. E., 79
Gaskell, E., 22, 43
genetic view, of family, 90-91
Gerber, E. W., American Woman in
    Sport, The, 145
Ginzburg, E., 132
girls, see daughters
Glick, P. C., 89, 102
Goeppert-Mayer, M., 32
Goode, T. L., 125
Goodenough, E. W., 60, 63
grade averages, self-perception and, 17
graduate schools, 113, 126
Graham, P., viii, 35, 47, 114, 115,
    116, 120
Greenberg, M., 57
Greenspan, A., 132

Griswold, E., 68n5
Guatamala, child-care in, 58
Gubernick, D., 17
guidance counselors, 108, 123, 137
Gutman, D., 56
Guttentag, M., 128

Hammer, D., 129
Harris, T. G., 86
Harris, P., vi
Harrison, B., 127
Hart, M., 143
Hartley, R. E., 83
Harvard Educational Review, 122
Harvard Gazette, 68n5
Harvard Law School, 34
Harvard Law School Bulletin, 50n7
Harvard University, women barred
    from, 108
Haslett, B., 17
health care, availability of, by sex, 78
Heilbrun, C., viii, 152-57
Helmreich, R., 138
Helson, R., 26, 33
Hennig, M., 27, 31, 33-34, 83, 143-144
    Managerial Woman, The, 25
Herzog, E., 52
Hetherington, M., 53, 101-102
high schools, *see* education (secondary)
history (American), perspective of, on
    women, 72-73
Hochschild, A., 38
Hodges, K. L. 141
Hoffman, D., 50n4
Hoffman, L. W., 42, 80, 81, 87n1, 96,
    103-104, 131, 138
Holbrook, *Parturition without Pain: A
    Code of Directions for Escaping
    the Primal Curse*, 110
Holstrom, L., 97, 98
homemakers
    compared to professional women,
    74-75
    self-perception of, 49
homosexuality, 68n5
Horner, M., 135, 136, 137, 138, 150n2
hours of work
    career opportunity and, 36-37, 116
    flexibility in, recommended, 47
    part-time occupations, 47, 123
How to Father (Dodson), 55
Hunt, H., 49
Hunter, G., 34
hunter-gatherer societies, 71-72

immigrants, daughters of, 28-29

impotence, 97
incompetence, women assume, 16-17
independence, *see* autonomy
industrialization, women's labor and,
    20, 73
"Infant Day Care Experience," 106n10
infant mortality, 72, 73, 78
infants, sex differences in, 79-80
inferiority, feelings of, among women,
    77
inheritance, law of, 60
insitutions
    infants reared in, 75-76
    social policies of, 36-37
International Women's Year
    Conference, 71
IQ
    birth order and, 103
    longitudinal variation in, 15-16
isolation
    of successful women, 34, 39, 45
    of women, 15, 70, 83

Jacklin, C. N., 87n1, 122, 125
Jardim, A., *Managerial Woman, The*,
    25
Jarvie, G. J., 129
Jayaratane, T., 46
Jewish culture, 61-62, 68n3
Joffee, C., 125
Johnson, M., 55

Kagan, J., 66, 81, 82, 105
Kangas, J., 16
Kanter, R. M., 38, 46
Karabenick, S. A., 150n1
Karle, I., 28
Kearsley, R., 105
Keith-Speigel, P., 50n4
Kitt, 82
Klein, A., 83
Kohen, J., "Divorce: Chance of a
    New Lifetime," 101
Kohlberg, L., 82, 83
Komarovsky, M., 105n2
Kotelchuck, M., 57, 58
Kotin, A., 101
Krebs, J., 141
Kukla, A., 140
Kundsin, R., 27, 31, 33, 34, 35, 39,
    45, 46, 48

labor
    division of, 54, 73, 91, 92, 93-94
    educational system and, 114
Labor Department (U.S.), 88-89

labor force
mothers in, 76, 89
wives in, 95-96
labor supply, competency and, 15
Lamb, M. E., 54, 58
Lamphere, L., 19, 71
Lancaster, J. B., 149
Landers, A., 78
law schools
admission policies of, 34-35
women in, 132
lawyers, 45
jobs as, for women, 24, 34-35, 36
per cent of women as, 23
leadership
in educational system, 117
femininity and, 18-19, 24
male socialization and, 24-25
political, by women, 26
Lein, L., 104
Lemkin, J., 66, 83
Leonard, M., 64
Lester, M., 58
Lever, J., 24
Levine, J. L., 59
Who Will Raise the Children, 76n1
Levitin, T. E., 124
Lewis, E., 33
Lewis, M., 65, 80
Lieberman, M. A., 148
life cycle
career and, 30-31, 152-153
identity and, 129
skills and, 14-15, 16
see also age
life-span, 72, 74
Lightfoot, S., vin, 114
Lipman-Blumen, J., 95, 105n1
Lloyd, C. B., 70, 73, 94
Lloyd, S., viii, 73, 121
Lowell, E. L., 134
luck, see attribution patterns
Luria, Z., 62
Lyberger, F. S., 126
Lynn, D. B., 56, 96, 97

McClelland, D., viii, 20, 134, 136
McDonagh, E., 26, 32
McHugh, M., 143
McLaughlin, 63
Maccoby, E. E., 87n1, 125
Male Machine, The (Feigen-Fasteau),
67n1
Managerial Woman, The (Hennig and
Jardim), 25

marriage
age at, 76, 82, 88, 89
feminist view of, 93-94
Parsons on, 92
satisfactions of, 96-97
sharing of power in, 96
of successful women, 40-41
marriage gradient, 99
Marshall, J. M., 150n1
masculinity
attributes of, 19-20, 74
father role and, 56
in male child, 63
occupation and, 123
traditional images of, 67n1
mastery, sense of, 18
Mastossian, J., 17
maternity leaves, 47
mathematicians and mathematics
sex and, 145-148
women as, 26
women barred from, 145
Mauser, B., 138
Meacham, C., 43
Mead, M., 57, 86
media, 154, 155
"lifestyles" in, 88
medical schools
women barred from, 24, 37
women students in, 26, 48, 130n1,
132
see also physicians
men
competence and, vi
competence women and, 138-139
educational system and, 115-116
effect on, of shared economic role,
96, 105n5
emotional repression in, 68n4
power and, 93-94, 121
role of, in genetic view, 91
role of, in sociological theory, 92
self-perception of, 16-17
status of, 60
Men and Masculinity (Pleck and
Sawyer), 67n1
Meredith, D., 54
Father Power, 67n1
Merton, R., 82
middle age, see life cycle
middle class(es)
daughter preference in, 61-62
family of, in change, 94-96
father/child relationships in, 57-58,
66-67

focus of study, vi
mother/daughter relationships in, 80
parental attitudes in, 62-63
race and, vi
see also class; working class
Miller, J. B., 149
Miller, S. M., 105n5
Minnhaar, G., 27, 33
mobility (geographic)
career opportunity and, 36
family and, 95, 97, 105n4
Monahan, L., 94n5
monogamy, 90
Morgan, S. W., 138
Moss, H. A., 79, 81
mother(s)
child-care role of, 57, 58, 70, 74-75, 76
of competent daughters, 85-86
competition of, with daughters, 65, 84
daughters and, 78-79, 82
employment and, 103-104
femininity model of, 83-84
immigrant, as role models, 27-28
of one-child family, 102-103
perception of, by daughters, 66-67, 82-83
preference for male child among, 77-78
separation from, 75-76
of successful women, 30-31, 83-84
vicarious achievement and, 94-95
Ms. magazine, 68n3

Nadelson, T., 105n5
Naegle, F. D., 62
Nash, J., 52
National Association for Non-Parents 106n8
National Bureau of Economic Research, 39
National Education Association, 115
National Organization for Women (NOW), 154
Task Force on Women in Words and Images 122
nepotism, career opportunity and, 35-36
New York Academy of Sciences (NYAS), 28, 45, 46
New York Times, 13, 23, 36, 44, 45, 71, 79, 88, 100, 102, 111, 112, 113, 116, 118, 132, 141
Ngai, S. Y., 105n4

Nochlin, L., 32, 45
Norris, N., 57
Norton, E., 22
Notable American Women, 26, 32
NOW, *see* National Organization for Women
Nye, F. I., 76, 104
NYAS, *see* New York Academy of Sciences (NYAS)

Oberlin College, 108
occupational structure
changes in, 47-48
divorce and, 100-101
formal constraints in, 34-37
position of women in, 23, 132, 133
vicarious achievement in, 94-95
O'Connell, E. J., 81
Oedipal conflict, 64
Of Woman Born (Rich), 77
Oglesby, C. A., 143, 144
Old-boy network, *see* protege system
O'Leary, V., 38
O Pioneers (Cather), 27
opportunity
as prerequisite of competence, 18
in sports, 144
Osofsky, J. D., 81
ostracization, *see* isolation
over-population, woman's labor and, 20, 74
overprotectiveness, 68

Papaneck, H., 95
Parsons, J. E., 141
Parsons, T., 54
on division of labor, 96
on marriage, 92
part-time occupations, 47, 123
Parturition without Pain: A Code of Directions for Escaping the Primal Curse (Holbrook), 110
paternity leave, 47
patrilineality, 60
Patterson, G. B., 124
Pederson, F., 56, 60
peer approval, need for, 83
Peer Perspective, 119
penis envy, 66
Peplau, L., 139
perception, *see* cognition and perception
Ph.D.'s, women and, 26, 32, 37, 117
physicians
family backgrounds of women as, 33-34

per cent of women as, 23
see also medical schools
Physiognomics (Aristotle), 142
pioneer, as metaphor of professional
    woman, 28, 40
Piscopia, E. L., 32
play and playfulness
    athletics and, 145
    of fathers, 58, 62
    see also athletes and athletics; games
Pleck, J., viii, 150n2
    Men and Masculinity, 67n1
police departments, women in, 41
politicians and politics, school boards
    and, 118
polygamy, 68n4
Poor, R., 47
population explosion, 47
Potter, R. G., 68n2
power
    femininity and, vii, 19
    as male characteristic, 93-94
    prerequisite for competency, 18-19
    sharing of, 96
    socialization and, 18, 82
pregnancy, employment and, 35
prejudice, educational institutions and,
    108
    see also discrimination
preschoolers, sex stereotypes among,
    127, 128-29
President's Council of Economic
    Advisors, 132
principals (of schools), 113, 114, 116,
    117, 119
prison guards, women as, 40
productivity, of schools, 118-119
promotion, attitudes and, 38, 44-45, 46
protege system, 39-40, 118, 156
Provenzano, F., 62
psychoanalysis
    father role and, 52
    mother role and, 84
    penis envy theory of, 66
public schools, employee policies in,
    34-35
Pyke, S. W., 125, 126

Quaker society, 20-21
"queen bee" syndrome, 46

race, *see* blacks
Radloff, 15
Rapoport, R. and R., 98
Ravitch, D., 107
readers, sexism in, 108, 122

Reed, A., 38
Reed, L., 140
Rich, A., *Of Woman Born*, 77
Ricks, F. A., 125, 126
Rindfuss, R. R., 59, 77
rivalry, in mother/daughter relation-
    ship, 83-84
Robson, K., 56
Rodgers, W. L., 96
Rodzinski, A., 95
Rodzinski, H., 95
role model(s)
    of successful women, 30-31, 43-44
    in women's education, 111, 113-114,
    120
    working mothers as, 103-104
role specialization, 96
Romer, N., 138
Rosaldo, M. Z., 19, 71
Rose, S., 140
Rosen, 50n6
Rosenbaum, R., 140
Rosenberg, C., 110, 111
Rosenberg, M., 17
Rosenkrantz, P. S., 19, 104
Rossi, A. S., 36, 40, 96
Rubin, J. Z., 62, 79
Ruble, D. N., 141
rural society, family life in, 70-71

Saario, T. N., 122
Safilios-Rothschild, C., 97
Sagi, P. C., 68n2
Sanger, M., 32, 38
Sawyer, J., *Men and Masculinity*, 67n1
Scheinfeld, A., 79
Schmuck, P., 118
Schneider, L., 115-116
sciences, backgrounds of women in,
    27-28
Scott, A., 68n5
Scott, A. C., 142, 143, 144
Sears, P. S., 100
secondary schools, *see* education
    (secondary)
segregation
    of sexes in education, 120
    in society, 148-149
self-confidence, 31, 130
self-esteem
    child-birth and, 56-57
    child-rearing and, 85-86
    competency and, 16-18, 21, 49, 130,
    141
    dominant attitude and, 45-46
    requirements for, 17, 18

singleness and, 99-100
selfishness, competency and, 15-16
self-hatred, 18-19
self-perception, of women, 16-17,
    19-20, 148
Sellers, M. J., 58
Sells, L., 145
separation, from mothers, 75-76
Serbin, L. A., 125, 150n4
sex differences
    in child-rearing, 65, 78-79, 80
    in children's games, 24
    classroom experience and, 123-126,
        142
    feminists on, 93
    genetics and, 90-91
    in infants, 79-80
    IQ and 15-16
    in parental attitudes, 62-63
    self-perception and, 16-17, 19
    skills and, 14, 146
    somatic, 144
sexism, 108, 111, 113-116, 122, 127
Sexton, P., *Feminized Male, The*, 112
sexuality
    father role and, 52, 53, 63-64
    female identity and, 82-83
    mother role and, 83-84
    role restrictions in, 68n5
    in work situations, 37, 38, 39, 40
Shaver, P., 121, 150n2
Sherman, J., 121, 150n2
siblings
    child-care by, 72
    IQ and, 103
Simpson, J., 35, 48
Single Blessedness (Adams), 99
singleness, 98-99
skill(s)
    children's games and, 24-25
    competency and, 13, 14-15
Sklar, K. K., 108
Small, A. W., 141
Smeal, E., 154
Smith H., 17
Smith M. B., 17, 18
Smith J., 97
Smith College, 115
Smith-Rosenberg, C., 110, 111, 148
socialization
    children's games as, 24, 25, 45, 131
    of women, 18, 44, 77, 82
social policies, of institutions, 36-37
Somerville, M., 33
sons
    fathers and, 52, 55

preference for, 59-61, 68n2, 77-79
    socialization of, 80-81, 85-86
Spelke, E., 58
Spence, J. T., 138
Spiegler, M. D., 139
spinsterhood, *see* singleness
Spitz, R., 75
Spock, B. M., 76
sports, *see* athletes and athletics:
    games; play and playfulness
Sportswoman, 145
Sprung, B., 127
Staines, G., 46
Stein, B., 47
Steinmann, A., 138
stereotypes and stereotyping
    child-care activities and, 67
    education and, 121, 122-123,
        124-125, 127, 128, 147
    foreign-born and, 28-29
    of men, 67n1
    of middle-class family, 94-95
    occupational choice and, 133
    of only child, 102-103
    successful women and, 30-31, 33,
        85-86
    of women workers, 37
Sternglanz, S. H., 126
Stewart, N. R., 123
stigma
    of childlessness, 102
    mathematics and, 145
    of single women, 98-99
    successful women and, 34
success (of women)
    academic, 83
    attribution of, 140
    black women and, 29
    defined, 23
    factors leading to, 26-29
    fear of, 121, 135, 136-137, 138,
        150n2
    motherhood and, 42-44
Sudia, C., 52
"supermom," concept of, 43
Swerdlow, M., 68n3

Tasch, R. J., 62
Tavris, C., 46
Taylor, S., 44
teachers (college and university), per
    cent of women as, 23, 114
teachers (elementary), women as,
    114-115
tests and testing, 134
    mathematics and, 146

sexual stereotypes in, 122-123
texts, sexism in, 111
Thematic Apperception Test, 134
Thomas, A. H., 123
Thomas, M. C., 109, 115
Thompson, C., 74
Thorndike, E. L., 90
Tidball, M. E., 115, 120
Tiger, L., 149
Time magazine, 40, 54, 59, 120
Tittle, C. K., 122, 123
Tobias, S., 147
token status, of women, 46
Tolkein, 157
tradition
  Biblical, 60, 63
  daughter role and, 54, 66, 82
  family structure and, 89
  father role and, 52-53, 54
  male child and, 60
  mother role and, 69-70, 77
  women and, 19, 20-21
training, *see* education
traits, sex relatedness of, 19
Tresemer, D., 137, 150n2
Trilling, L., 153
Trivers, R. L., 56
Trojan Women, The, 156
Trollope, Frances, 30
Turner, B. G., 29
Tyack, D., viii, 108, 113, 114, 118

Ullian, D. Z., 83
underachievement, concern for,
  112-113
unemployment, 41
United Nations Food and Agriculture
  Organization, 78
universities, *see* colleges and
  universities
University of California (Berkeley), 145

value(s)
  of children, 71, 72, 73
  labor and, 15, 20, 71
  mother role, 76
  socialization and, 18
Vaughter, R., 17
Veroff, J., 105n2
vicarious achievement, 94-95
virtue, *see* value(s)
visual-spatial skills, 146
vocational interest tests, 123
Vogel, S. R., 19, 104
vulnerability, 18, 84

Wallace, P., 39
Wallston, B., 96, 104
Walsh, M. R., viii, 49
Walstedt, J., viii
Waring, G., 20
Weiner, B., 140
Weingarten, K., 104, 105n6
Weinraub, M., 65, 80
Wiess, S., 52
Westoff, C. F., 59, 68n2, 77
White, R., 14, 15
Whiting, B. B., 70, 72, 105n7
Whiting, J. W., 68n4
Who's Who in American Women, 120
Who Will Raise the Children (Levine),
  67n1
Winchell, R., 121
Wolfe, D. M. 96
women
  cross cultural analysis of, 70-74
  depression in, 15-16
  educational system and, 108-109,
    113-115, 120
  factors leading to achievement by,
    26-29
  historical perspectives on, 72-73,
    108-110
  occupational structure and, 23, 89
  relationships among, 45-46, 77
  role of, in genetic view, 91
  role of, in sociological theory,
    92-93, 96-97
  self-perception of, 16-17
  socialization of, 18, 24-25
  status of, 77
  success of, 22-23
Women's Movement, 93, 97
women's groups, 148-149, 150n5
Women Sports, 145
Woolf, V., 155
working class(es)
  child-care in, 104
  father's absence in, 53
  see also class; middle class(es)
World War II, 113
  absent fathers in, 52
  child-centered family and, 75
  women's labor and, 76
Wylie, P. C., 17
Wyrick, W., *American Woman in
  Sport, The*, 145

Zelazo, P., 105

The Competent Woman

Perspectives on Development

Rosalind C. Barnett and
Grace K. Baruch

With an Afterword by Carolyn G. Heilbrun

A comprehensive and up-to-date review of the literature on women's struggle to develop and exercise competence. The focus on competence—*defined as the ability to interact effectively with the environment*—provides a powerful starting point for an analysis of the major factors influencing the development of competence throughout the life cycle.

Dr. Barnett and Dr. Baruch bring together a wide variety of sources, both technical and anecdotal, spanning many disciplines. *The Competent Woman* discusses the nature of competence (Chapter 1) and reviews what is known about successful women (Chapter 2). The authors then discuss family influences, specifically the influence of fathers (Chapter 3), mothers (Chapter 4), and differing marital and family patterns (Chapter 5). The influence of schools is analyzed in Chapter 6. Chapter 7 looks at attitudes and behavior, including the literature on attributions.

In the Afterword, Carolyn Heilbrun, Professor of English at Columbia University, confronts the problems faced by women, praising the fairness and brutal honesty with which the authors present both the costs and rewards of accomplishment.

The Competent Woman is of special value not only to women but also to men who want to understand the issues confronting the women in their lives—wives, daughters, students, and colleagues.